NEW DIRECTIONS FOR STUDENT SERVICES

Using Professional Standards in Student Affairs

William A. Bryan
University of North Carolina

Roger B. Winston, Jr.
University of Georgia, Athens

Theodore K. Miller
University of Georgia, Athens

EDITORS

Number 53, Spring 1991

JOSSEY-BASS INC., PUBLISHERS
San Francisco

USING PROFESSIONAL STANDARDS IN STUDENT AFFAIRS
William A. Bryan, Roger B. Winston, Jr., Theodore K. Miller (eds.)
New Directions for Student Services, no. 53
Margaret J. Barr, Editor-in-Chief
M. Lee Upcraft, Associate Editor

Microfilm copies of issues and articles are available in 16mm and 35mm, as well as microfiche in 105mm, through University Microfilms Inc., 300 North Zeeb Road, Ann Arbor, Michigan 48106.

LC 85-644751 ISSN 0164-7970 ISBN 1-55542-797-9

NEW DIRECTIONS FOR STUDENT SERVICES is part of The Jossey-Bass Higher and Adult Education Series and is published quarterly by Jossey-Bass Inc., Publishers (publication number USPS 449-070). Second-class postage paid at San Francisco, California, and at additional mailing offices. Postmaster: Send address changes to Jossey-Bass Inc., Publishers, 350 Sansome Street, San Francisco, California 94104.

EDITORIAL CORRESPONDENCE should be sent to the Editor-in-Chief, Margaret J. Barr, Sadler Hall, Texas Christian University, Fort Worth, Texas 76129.

Cover photograph by Wernher Krutein/PHOTOVAULT © 1990.

Printed on acid-free paper in the United States of America.

Contents

Editors' Notes

With the growing interest in determining institutional effectiveness and the push toward accountability through outcomes assessment and budgetary monitoring systems, the American higher education community has been called upon by various segments of the population to justify its existence, or to at least demonstrate that students benefit from having attended its institutions. Student affairs divisions have not been exempt from this call to demonstrate competence and relevance to the educational mission.

Because the student affairs practice as a field staffed by professionals—rather than as a collection of well-meaning amateurs principally skilled at using common sense and intuition—is still relatively young, there have been few extra-institutional reference points available to measure effectiveness or justify practices. Slightly over a decade ago, however, professional student affairs associations, representing many functional areas, realized that if the field was to continue its development as a profession, there must be generally accepted standards for determining minimally adequate programs and services. In response to this need, the Council for the Advancement of Standards for Student Services/Development Programs (CAS) was formed in 1979. In 1986 and 1987, CAS published standards and guidelines for seventeen functional work areas in student affairs as a cooperative venture among twenty-two professional associations. In 1988, CAS published self-assessment guides, which are operational versions of *CAS Standards and Guidelines* designed for practitioners to use in program development or accreditation self-studies. For the first time, these documents outlined a formalized process for reviewing the effectiveness of student affairs work based on minimal criteria.

Clearly, for these standards and other professional standards to be applied effectively, there must be adequate understanding of how standards can improve planning, program development, preparation for accreditation activities, and self-studies, as well as adequate faculty awareness of the depth of student development activities and the impact of cocurricular programs on the modern campus. We strongly believe that professional standards make a difference when they are used and practiced and that they are a pathway to excellence.

This volume, *Using Professional Standards in Student Affairs,* is designed to assist student affairs professionals in becoming more knowledgeable about professional standards, especially the CAS standards, and to sensitize them to some of the important issues and concerns associated with the application of standards. It has been five years since the initial publication of *CAS Standards and Guidelines.* During that interval many creative and utilitarian applications of the standards have been developed; this volume describes some of these applications with the aim of encouraging more practitioners to scrutinize existing programs and practices in order to determine how well they are meeting student needs and addressing institutional goals. Specific applications in the areas of program planning, self-study, program review, and staff and program evaluation are detailed.

This volume is intended for student affairs professionals in general, and for chief student affairs officers and program directors in particular. It can also be useful in institutional planning and assessment efforts when student affairs personnel are called upon to justify their programs and services. It can provide valuable information regarding standards implementation, especially for institutions that are preparing to undertake self-studies for accreditation purposes. The ultimate tests of the usefulness of standards, however, must be how well they promote programs and services that address student needs, contribute to student education, and further the mission of the institution.

In Chapter One, Phyllis Mable explores the concept of professional standards and its relationships to accreditation, credentialing, and other regulatory functions are elucidated. She provides a historical review of the development of the student affairs profession and the adoption of a broad-base set of standards. The development of *CAS Standards and Guidelines* and *CAS Self Assessment Guides* is highlighted along with other student affairs standards.

Barbara Jacoby and William L. Thomas, Jr., in Chapter Two, discuss the use and value of standards and interpretive guidelines as the basis of self-studies mandated by regional accrediting associations and by student affairs associations. They provide specific examples of the use of standards in the accreditation process and review potential issues and problems surrounding this use of standards.

In Chapter Three, William A. Bryan and Richard H. Mullendore discuss the use of *CAS Standards and Guidelines* to monitor performance and to develop plans for improving programs and services with students. Strategies for using the standards and guidelines as program-planning tools within departments of a student affairs division, as well as their use as part of a division's long-range planning, are explained. Also, a process of annual program review based on CAS standards is proffered.

Theodore K. Miller, in Chapter Four, describes and critiques the three professional preparation tracts—counseling, administrative, and developmental—and discusses the accreditation process for academic programs through the Council for the Accreditation of Counseling and Other Related Educational Programs. This chapter's primary focus is on standards for professional preparation, though it touches on the educational potential of statements of ethical standards and standards of professional practice.

In Chapter Five, Roger B. Winston, Jr., and William S. Moore define outcomes assessment in a student affairs context and present a model for conceptualizing the enterprise. The use of CAS standards in outcomes assessment is highlighted, and methodological issues inherent to outcomes assessment are addressed. A selection of instruments and other measurement techniques that may be useful in outcomes assessment are presented.

Joseph M. Marron, in Chapter Six, describes the uses of *CAS Standards and Guidelines* by a number of colleges and universities. Issues related to the use of standards are explored, and strengths and weaknesses in the present approaches are discussed.

William A. Bryan
Roger B. Winston, Jr.
Theodore K. Miller
Editors

William A. Bryan is vice-chancellor for student affairs at the University of North Carolina, Wilmington, and professor of educational design and management. He has worked as a student affairs administrator since 1961 and has served as a chief student affairs officer for the past thirteen years.

Roger B. Winston, Jr., is professor in the Student Personnel in Higher Education Program in the Department of Counseling and Human Development Services at the University of Georgia, Athens. He was a member of the CAS Board of Directors from 1982 to 1988. His research interests have centered on the measurement of student psychosocial development and of higher education environments.

Theodore K. Miller is professor of education and coordinator of the Student Personnel in Higher Education Program in the Department of Counseling and Human Development Services at the University of Georgia, Athens. He has been actively involved in the development and applications of professional standards during the past decade. He chaired the American College Personnel Association Task Force that drafted the first student affairs preparation standards in 1979. He was a founding member of CAS and its president from 1979 to 1989.

A collaborative profession-wide effort has resulted in the establishment of professional standards of practice in student services and student development programs. These standards have the capacity to contribute in many ways to the improvement of undergraduate education. The standards recognize the value of out-of-class experience as a valid component of student development and have great utility for enhancing self-study processes.

Professional Standards: An Introduction and Historical Perspective

Phyllis Mable

Over the years, student services and development programs have gained in stature, vision, and recognition as an essential part of higher education's mission. However, one important element was missing until very recently, that is, a set of comprehensive standards for program and staff development and program evaluation, self-study, and accreditation. During the past decade, student affairs professionals have become increasingly aware of the need for a well-defined set of standards for student services and development programs. A primary reason for this awareness is the efforts of some twenty student services professional associations, which collaborated in establishing the Council for the Advancement of Standards for Student Services/Development Programs (CAS). These professional associations have jointly proposed standards for specific functional areas, thereby providing a valuable service for student service practitioners who strive to meet the academic and personal developmental needs of college students. As the standards and guidelines designed and developed by CAS have gained increasing recognition and acceptance, the purpose and utility of student services and development programs have continued to expand. Consequently, the concept of a quality undergraduate education has also expanded—from subject-matter mastery as the sole goal to acquisition of the skills and practical understandings essential to achieving successful and effective lives in terms of both worth *and* work.

This chapter explores the concept of professional standards and its relationships to accreditation, credentialing, and other regulatory functions.

A historical review of the development of the student affairs profession and the ultimate adoption of a broad-base set of standards is provided. In particular, the development of *CAS Standards and Guidelines* and *CAS Self Assessment Guides* is highlighted along with recognition of other student affairs standards that also exist.

Development of Professional Standards: A Perspective

To the credit of American higher education, the primary approach to evaluation and control is a strong emphasis on self-regulation. In the words of Kells (1983, p. 9), self-regulation means "peer professional and institutional pressure to meet generally accepted standards and to improve through self-assessment and periodic peer review." Self-regulation has developed over the years as professionals have evaluated their experiences and made improvements in accordance with appropriate reviews. Student affairs professionals and colleagues have been anxious to collaborate through their professional associations and to create standards for the functional areas that typically fall under their jurisdiction. The opportunity to establish a total student development climate within student cultures has been a high priority.

However, professional standards and accreditation in the student affairs arena have a relationship that requires further, more systematic nurturance. The potential for this relationship exists primarily in the self-study process, since the use of the professional standards established by the collaborative efforts of student affairs associations is voluntary in nature. Throughout the self-study process, services and development programs in student affairs are expected to reflect institutional goals and purposes. These programs should serve both students and the institution effectively, so that the campus culture supports student development and the notion that every part of a student's educational experience matters. As standards prepared by student affairs professional associations are utilized, the purposes of self-study, such as defined and explained by Kells (1983, p. 15), are enhanced: "Self-study processes are intended to help institutions and programs improve. . . . Self-study processes should result in the further incorporation into the life of the institution or program of ongoing, useful, institutional research and self-analysis. . . . Self-study processes should precede and should be the firm foundation for all planning efforts."

The self-study process forms the basis for accrediting processes and procedures. Furthermore, professional standards and guidelines are the essence of self-study. Standards should offer clear statements of what student services and development programs must provide. Without these statements of criteria to judge against, it is difficult to determine exactly how effective and appropriate the services and programs really are. However, a self-study based on selected standards does much more than simply identify problems. The posture of accreditation has changed from a prescriptive thrust to one that challenges the institution to learn more about itself and to design changes and improvements based on substantial probes into the goals and accomplishments of its services and programs.

As mentioned previously, a number of initiatives have been taken to create standards and guidelines in specific student affairs functional areas. Examples of some of these initiatives include the following. In 1970, guidelines were written for university and college counseling centers by a special task force of counseling center directors. The International Association of Counseling Services (1982) currently utilizes these standards for accreditation of university and college counseling services. In 1979, the National Association of College and University Food Services (1982) completed a self-study calling for standards to assess levels of operational performance provided by college and university food services. The National Intramural-Recreational Sports Association (NIRSA) adopted collegiate recreational sports standards in 1981. As explained in the NIRSA (1989, p. 3) document, "The Standards can be used for program development, program evaluation, and comparison of institutions as they reflect elements of form, substance and philosophy that are essential to a quality lifestyle for students as it relates to the recreational sports experience." The Association of College and University Housing Officers-International adopted standards in 1985 that have utility for staff and graduate educational programs, accreditation self-studies, collegiate community information projects, and assistance to outside agencies concerned with student housing.

The American College Health Association (1977) first published standards and practices for college health programs in 1964 and will soon publish the fifth edition of *Recommended Standards and Practices for a College Health Program,* a volume that serves as a guide for providing and assessing essential student health services. In 1981, the National Association for Foreign Student Affairs published a set of self-regulation principles for international educational exchange, which can be used to assess current programs and guide institutional planning to improve services on the basis of self-study. Beginning in 1979, the American Council on Education ([ACE] 1979, 1988) prepared guidelines for colleges and universities on nine topics: (1) Policy Guidelines for Refund of Student Charges, (2) Joint Statement on Principles of Good Practice in College Admissions and Recruitment, (3) Collegiate Athletics Policy Statements, (4) Joint Statement on Transfer and Award of Academic Credits, (5) Joint Statement on Standards of Satisfactory Academic Progress to Maintain Financial Aid Eligibility, (6) Academic Integrity and Athletic Eligibility, (7) Confidentiality of College and University Faculty Personnel Files: Its Appropriate Role in Institutional Affairs, (8) Statement on Access to and Disclosures from Employee Records, and (9) Statement on Educational Diversity, Equality, and Quality.

In 1984, ACE prepared a series of five resource documents all in the interest of self-regulation initiatives: (1) Principles for Developing Credit-

Based Instructional Programs with a Business, Industry, or other Non-Collegiate Organization, (2) Achieving Reasonable Campus Security, (3) Student Athletic Drug-Testing Programs, (4) Higher Education and Research Entrepreneurship: Conflicts Among Interests, and (5) Alcohol and Other Substance Abuse: Resources for Institutional Action. The ACE Office on Self-Regulation Initiatives also provides "self-regulatory assistance on various issues of differing institutional concern and commonality" (ACE, 1984, inside cover). Finally, in 1988, the National Association of State Universities and Land Grant Colleges published the fundamental *Statement of Principles on Student Outcomes Assessment*. However, only two of the regional institutional accrediting bodies endorsed by the Council on Postsecondary Accreditation (COPA) have standards pertaining to students and student development services: Northwest Association of Schools and Colleges (1988) and Southern Association of Colleges and Schools (1989–1990).

Professional Standards in Student Affairs: Relationship to Accreditation

Professional standards provide scope and shape to total student development via specific plans, perspectives, and realistic forms of self-regulation that are relatively free from outside intervention. Thoughtful professionals know that students are best served through quality educational service and program performance delivery tempered with wisdom, justice, and imagination. Professional standards (essentials) and guidelines (recommendations) provide excellent supports to guide the process of student development. Without such standards, the practice of student affairs is too often taken for granted by institutional officials who either place it high in importance but have little notion of what outcomes to expect or else turn their backs on student life and have little interest in the value of out-of-class learning and its contribution to student performance and education.

Over the years, a combination of curricular and cocurricular activity has seldom been recognized and defined in terms of institutional effectiveness. Student affairs has often been viewed as a "frill," peripheral to the educational mission, even though the out-of-class experiences of students have an enormous influence on their attempts to establish lives filled with direction and innovation. Ernest L. Boyer (1987, p. 218) concluded that "today's undergraduates urgently need to see the relationship between what they learn and how they live." As the student affairs dimension becomes a more focused part of the higher education enterprise, principles must be established to guide and assess the adequacy of student services and development programs. If student affairs professionals do not define these connecting principles, then the various aspects of campus life will be unconnected, or, worse yet, the gaps filled in ways that fail to involve or encourage unified efforts. The essentials of student affairs services and development programs are extremely important, first and foremost to students struggling to become focused, competent, and committed human beings who experience a sense of wholeness from putting their lives in perspective.

Fortunately, the field of student affairs has established professional standards for many of its functional areas and has built a foundation for shaping the substance of its programs. Consequently, the various parts of student life are beginning to connect, each with a specific role in the learning community. In turn, students are expected and challenged to become involved and to learn in accordance with clearly defined and articulated goals and objectives. In addition, the role of student affairs in higher education as a whole is becoming increasingly viable, and its value can increase as students establish their identities in the knowledge, skills, and attitudes integrated in cocurricular initiatives. Through the concept of professional standards, the role and function of student affairs in undergraduate education are enhanced, understood, accomplished, and evaluated. As Winston and Moore (this volume) point out, the use of standards is a double-edged sword. Most standards require an evaluation of the effectiveness of services and programs provided; therefore, student affairs becomes more accountable.

However, now that professional standards are in place, how are they related to accreditation? According to the handbook published by COPA (1988, p. 3), "Accreditation is a system for recognizing educational institutions and professional programs affiliated with those institutions for a level of performance, integrity, and quality which entitles them to the confidence of the educational community and the public they serve. In the United States, this recognition is extended primarily through nongovernmental, voluntary institutional or professional associations. These groups establish criteria for accreditation, arrange site visits, evaluate those institutions and professional groups which desire accredited status, and publicly designate those which meet their criteria."

Accreditation both ensures program or institutional quality and encourages improvement. Today, much concern and interest are expressed for strengthening undergraduate education. Accreditation promotes a basis for shaping the nature of that education and points out the necessity for enchancing the levels of knowledge and skills among students. This system of voluntary evaluation calls for a personal commitment to quality, with self-examination playing an essential role in the regulating process and outcome.

Accreditation generally urges the independence of institutions and programs and encourages positive innovation. Thus, professional standards in student affairs can be used in analytical self-studies to review the goals of the student affairs program and its functional areas. Such studies can effectively determine the extent of success in accomplishing goals and evaluating learning by way of student outcomes based on the goals. If professional standards provide thoughtful statements about what each functional area is expected to provide, then the extent to which services and development programs are being accomplished and enhanced can more readily be determined. Accreditation processes and procedures are increasingly being focused on results and learning outcomes, as opposed to emphasizing resources. While the recognized institutional accrediting bodies have not required their constituent institutions to adhere to professional standards established by student affairs professional associations, they can elect to encourage their member institutions to do so. Together with institutions and programs, accrediting bodies are responsible for enhancing and improving higher education. Thus, professional standards can help define the mission and goals necessary for identifying intellectual educational outcomes.

It is important to remember the ultimate purpose of program goals, standards, and accreditation processes. Above all, student affairs practitioners are engaged in the business of helping students improve their lives. Professional standards can both enable and encourage institutions to do something specific and significant *for students.* Standards can promote the value of student affairs, as well as its distinctiveness, image, and reputation.

Professional standards can provide the challenge that student services and development programs need to contribute to each student's education and personal growth, to encourage students' involvement in learning and persistence in successfully completing educational goals, and to support their initiatives in fulfilling adult roles. Standards influence the vision, perspective, and skills gleaned from an effective institution, such as the cultivation of confidence and self-esteem, community care and service, open-mindedness, tolerance, creative and critical thinking, and a capacity for empathy and aesthetic expression. Standards also demand a deep analysis and clear account of what is expected for both student services and development programs and student performance.

Finally, accreditation is designed to fulfill the dual purposes of quality assurance and institutional and program improvement, and to provide the public with an understanding of institutions that have voluntarily participated in planned activities to improve education. Marjorie Pace Lenn (1987, p. 49) described accreditation as "an internalized activity that is a direct, self-regulatory creation of the academic and professional education communities and is administered by nongovernmental associations of institutions, programs, and professionals in particular fields." In the case of credentialing and certification, such processes clearly apply only to individuals. Credentials certainly evidence a mastery of knowledge and skills by an individual, and certification provides recognition to an individual who meets specific qualifications and who voluntarily seeks recognition. Unfortunately, such official recognition is not currently available for institutions and programs since there is no direct connection between professional standards in student affairs and the regional institutional accrediting bodies. However, student services and development programs can use the standards as criteria for accreditation-related self-studies, as well as to promote the establishment, improvement, and involvement of student affairs and total student development as part of the institution's mission and goals. It is time to address issues and ideas that truly help students to seek an identity that gives meaning and purpose to their existence.

Council for the Advancement of Standards: Its Beginning

In addition to the aforementioned standards, guidelines, and principles, CAS has made a commitment to maintain and improve quality in student services and development programs and to effect desirable changes. The initial CAS standards and guidelines were published in 1986 and represented over six years of initiative and effort by professionals involved in twenty-two professional associations.

In June 1979, a meeting of student affairs professional association representatives was held to consider the desirability and feasibility of establishing professional standards and accreditation programs in student affairs. This meeting was indeed a milestone as it evidenced the need for an interassociation approach to addressing standards in student services and development programs, as well as an interest in accreditation initiatives. Subsequently, an invitational conference was held in October 1979 to bring together representatives from as many interested student services associations as possible. Their goal was to examine accreditation as a quality-assurance function for the student affairs profession, both for academic professional preparation programs and functional areas for the practice of student services. Primary considerations also included the role of standards for preparation and practice in the profession and an interassociation consortium on accreditation. The conference produced strong support for an interassociation entity, which eventually became the Council for the Advancement of Standards for Student Services/Development Programs. The initiative gained momentum with the appointment of task forces to prepare materials for an organizational meeting in January 1980. These materials included bylaws, a plan for collection and unification of standards from associations, public relations, future task forces, a collection of current professional standards, and a plan for the January 1980 organization meeting.

Prior to the establishment of CAS, the Association for Counselor Education and Supervision proposed standards for counselor education in 1973, which were adopted by the American Personnel and Guidance Association in 1977. The American College Personnel Association reviewed and revised these standards in 1979 in an attempt to make them more relevant to the special needs of college student affairs preparation programs. A comprehensive discussion of these and subsequent events associated with standards of professional preparation is in Miller (this volume).

As the professional standards development initiative progressed, the

CAS member associations recognized that accreditation could be granted only through established sources of authority. COPA (1988, p. 4) is a "non-governmental organization that works to foster and facilitate the role of accrediting bodies in promoting and insuring the quality and diversity of American postsecondary education," and COPA is our source of authority. COPA is an umbrella organization that represents a merger of existing accrediting agencies, including the Federation of Regional Accrediting Bodies and the Council for Specialized Accrediting Agencies. COPA recognizes, coordinates, and reviews the efforts of the regional and specialized accrediting agencies in higher/postsecondary education, and its authority comes from the membership of college and university presidents. COPA was formed in 1975, and it has worked to foster and facilitate the benefits of accreditation through development of criteria and guidelines for assessing educational effectiveness and through continuous self-study and review.

Thus, standards and guidelines became a primary interest for student affairs professionals, especially as they worked diligently to shape their profession and to have it recognized by higher education as contributing to each student's education and growth through services and development programs. The accreditation of student affairs programs is largely in the hands of the regional institutional accrediting bodies of CPA, as influenced by institutional presidents and student affairs leaders and professional associations who urge the use of student affairs standards for accreditation purposes. The organizational structure adopted by CAS provided all professional associations with an interest in college student services an opportunity to prepare professional standards for practice and preparation alike. Through this initiative, the autonomy and integrity of the individual professional associations were preserved, and yet the values, programs, and theories of the student affairs profession came to be more fully recognized, accepted, and implemented throughout all of higher education.

The original bylaws of CAS (1980) stated the council's purposes:

> The Council for the Advancement of Standards for Student Development/Services Programs (hereinafter "Council") is a non-profit corporation organized for the purpose of promoting cooperative interassociation efforts to establish and adopt professional standards for student development/services programs and for the preparation of professionals for these fields, including, but not limited to, the following:
>
> (a) To encourage the regional and specialized accreditation agencies to utilize student development/services standards prepared by a consolidated effort of professionals in these fields;
> (b) To provide standards and professional consultation to assist institutions of higher education in the evaluation and improvement of their student development/services programs;

(c) To provide written standards and professional consultation to assist institutions of higher education in the evaluation and improvement of professional preparation programs in the student development/services areas;
(d) To increase administrators, faculty and practicum professionals' awareness of the importance of professional standards as a guide for these student development/services program areas and activities; and
(e) To carry out such other functions as are necessary to develop such professional standards and to have them adopted and implemented by both accreditation agencies and institutions of higher education [pp. 1-2].

As the purposes of CAS became more focused, significant, and realistic, the purposes in the bylaws (CAS, 1988) were shaped to reflect the improvement and advancement of student services and development programs. The bylaws have also promoted more cooperative interassociation efforts to improve the quality of services offered to students by establishing, adopting, and recommending professional standards for student services and development programs and for professional preparation.

CAS Standards and Guidelines enables institutions to better assess, study, and evaluate their student services and development programs and to improve and utilize them more fully. The standards and guidelines contain many possibilities for enhancing the notion of exactly what students should learn and become as they engage in the process of educating themselves for careers as well as for life's many opportunities and involvements. Presently, standards and guidelines exist for nineteen functional areas and for preparation programs. During the coming years, CAS plans to review and revise present standards based on use and experience and will add standards and guidelines for functional areas not previously addressed. CAS follows a concentrated and comprehensive process that ensures interested member associations have adequate involvement before the council adopts or amends standards and guidelines for a particular functional area. Thus, since its establishment over a decade ago, with the involvement of many individuals from its member associations, CAS continues to help define and shape the future of the profession.

Development of the CAS Standards and Self-Assessment Guides

CAS was established to develop a "definition" of our profession—a series of goals that practitioners can strive to meet in the programs of their colleges and universities. However, these standards and guidelines exist not as an end in themselves but rather as aids to help practitioners focus on their professional goals of providing substance and direction to the out-of-class experiences of students who are seeking to establish identity and involvement in their lives. CAS was formally established in 1979 when articles of incorporation as a not-for-profit organization were filed in Washington, D.C. Full voting membership on the council was opened to all national-level professional associations related to student services and development programs, with each association authorized to appoint a director and alternate director to the CAS board. Each member association was allotted one vote, and nonvoting associate membership was provided to regional associations. Additionally, two public directors with voting privileges were appointed. When *CAS Standards and Guidelines* was published in 1986, there were twenty member associations and two associate member associations.

As noted previously, nineteen functional area standards currently exist, with the recent addition of standards and guidelines for Women Student Programs and Services in 1989 and Alcohol and Other Drug Programs in 1990. The standards and guidelines of each CAS functional area incorporated a set of general standards, which were identified as common for all functions. Various CAS member associations identified functional areas and initiated drafts of standards for areas in which they had interest and expertise. CAS committees received the various proposed drafts and created a unified, single document for each functional area. Next, the CAS Executive Committee edited, revised, and consolidated each *unified* draft and circulated them through member associations for review and comment.

The resulting feedback process resulted in additional amendments to the drafts, which were then put before the CAS Board of Directors for consideration. A two-thirds affirmative vote by member associations and public directors was required for CAS adoption of each standard, which then became eligible for public dissemination and comment. Functional area standards and guidelines adopted by the council were submitted to two or more nationally recognized experts in the functional area and distributed widely within the professional and higher education community. Based on the feedback received, specific suggestions for revisions were considered by the CAS Executive Committee. Amendment proposals and changes were referred to the council, with the Board of Directors making final decisions about amendments on the basis of a two-thirds majority vote.

A CAS standards review and revision process was begun in 1989, three years after the publication of the original CAS document, for purposes of bringing all functional area standards into "state-of-the-art" form. This process will take approximately six years to complete. A process for developing new CAS standards is also in place. Both processes encourage the involvement of professional associations, functional area experts, and CAS directors and alternates in standards development. The many steps in both protocols require careful, thorough, and comprehensive treatment of all standards development efforts, a process that is a source of professional pride for those involved and one that will enhance the quality and improvement of undergraduate education in America.

Professionals who use *CAS Standards and Guidelines* (CAS, 1986) must understand the difference between the two types of elements involved. Standards reflect the *minimum essential elements* relevant to student services and development programs, whereas guidelines represent *recommended elements.* The standards use the auxiliary verbs *must* and *shall* and appear in boldface type in the 1986 document and in *CAS Self Assessment Guides* (Miller, Thomas, Looney, and Yerian, 1989). Guidelines use *should* and *may* as auxiliary verbs and are intended to provide amplification and interpretation of standards through the use of examples and explanations. The standards in the CAS documents are essential components of an acceptable student services/development program, but they do not necessarily describe state-of-the-art practice. Perhaps the most significant aspect of the CAS process is the establishment of standards and guidelines that were developed through collaborative, consensus-taking efforts among member associations and that involve large numbers of professional practitioners. Another noteworthy feature is the role of the general standards, which must be used in conjunction with the standards and guidelines for each functional area. The standards for each functional area are a continuation of the general standards, and they are guided by the context and direction of them. Only those functional area standards consistent with the mission and structure of a particular institution should be used in evaluation efforts. However, functional area standards should be addressed even when separate administrative units do not exist for the area under scrutiny, for example, when one professional in a small college is responsible for several student affairs functions.

As use of *CAS Standards and Guidelines* began to materialize, the CAS directors recognized the need for a self-assessment procedure designed to operationalize the standards and guidelines. Thus, *CAS Self Assessment Guides* (Miller, Thomas, Looney, and Yerian, 1988) enables professionals to determine the extent and nature of their compliance with each standard component. Professionals are asked to consider involvement, accomplishment, and investment in each standard and to document the effectiveness of compliance with specific evidence that supports the judgments of quality made by committees and individuals. Student affairs professionals who engage in this experience gain insight about the programs for which they are responsible, especially as the programs contribute to student learning. Gaps are readily identified and analyzed. *CAS Self Assessment Guides* presents criterion measures in an easily used rating and worksheet format that is clearly connected to the standards.

Professionals doing self-studies can quickly gain an informed and comprehensive understanding of each functional area's strengths and deficiencies and will be able to identify needed changes, improvements, and enhancements based on documented analysis. The worksheet format requires a challenging depth of thought, as assessment criteria related to standards are noted with appropriate compliance judgments. The prescriptions for identifying and summarizing evaluation evidence, describing discrepancies between assessment criteria and actual program practice, delineating required corrective actions, and recommending special actions for program enhancement provide a thorough format for self-study, improvement, and accreditation purposes.

Influence of Standards on the Profession and Higher Education

Considering the amount of work and thought involved in their development, professional standards in student affairs are a significant accomplishment. *CAS Standards and Guidelines* provides a much-needed focus, direction, and perspective to student affairs practice. They also proffer a guiding vision of substance and integrity and stable and permanent criteria against which to measure out-of-class education, involvement, and learning pertaining to student development. They enable the student affairs practice to become more significant, valid, and credible in its quest to graduate from service programs of convenience to programs that reflect conviction, purpose, and persuasion. Over time, as *CAS Standards and Guidelines* is reviewed and revised, student affairs will continue to enhance the quality of academic life and institutional purpose. The value of the student affairs practice will be increasingly recognized as the meaning and coherence of education become clear in the minds and hearts of students, faculty, and administrators. Student affairs is indeed monitoring its own opportunities and obligations.

Warren Byran Martin (1982, p. 99) effectively stated the notion that students learn more outside the classroom than within: "Because the nonacademic side of campus life is so important, a college of character will give as much attention to student life—to cultural programs, counseling services, intramural athletics, art, music, and drama—as to any academic dimensions of campus life." How will this challenge affect student affairs professionals as they strive for clarity of purpose, clarity of function, and clarity of vision? *CAS Standards and Guidelines* expresses as clearly as possible the educational functions and purposes of student services and development programs, and they have a rationale based on theory, principle, practice, and institutional mission. These standards and guidelines place the *musts* and *shoulds* solidly within the framework of expectations and visions that are wisely chosen.

The CAS process points to standards and values that are absolutely essential for student learning. They challenge student affairs professionals to be educational leaders and to be distinctive and purposeful, especially as *CAS Self Assessment Guides* opens doors for more precise evaluation and action, as well as a sharper vision of student learning and development. Thus, *CAS Standards and Guidelines* has become a force for change, with a basic core of convictions from which student services and development programs gain synergy and direction for the next decade and beyond.

References

American College Health Association (ACHA). *Recommended Standards and Practices for a College Health Program.* Washington, D.C.: ACHA, 1977.

American Council on Education (ACE). *Resource Documents and Self-Regulation Guidelines.* Washington, D.C.: ACE, 1979.

American Council on Education. *Resource Documents and Self-Regulation Guidelines.* Washington, D.C.: ACE, 1984.

American Council on Education. *Self-Regulation Initiatives: Resource Documents for Colleges and Universities.* Washington, D.C.: ACE, 1988.

Association for Counselor Education and Supervision (ACES). *Standards for the Preparation of Counselors and Other Personnel Services Specialists at the Masters Degree Level.* Washington, D.C.: ACES, 1973.

Association of College and University Housing Officers-International (ACUHO-I). *Statement of Standards.* Columbus, Ohio: ACUHO-I, 1985.

Boyer, E. L. *College, the Undergraduate Experience in America.* New York: Harper & Row, 1987.

Council for the Advancement of Standards for Student Services/Development Programs (CAS). *Bylaws for the Council for the Advancement of Standards for Student Services/Development Programs.* Washington, D.C.: CAS, 1980.

Council for the Advancement of Standards for Student Services/Development Programs. *CAS Standards and Guidelines for Student Services/Development Programs.* Washington, D.C.: CAS, 1986.

Council for the Advancement of Standards for Student Services/Development Programs. *Bylaws for the Council for the Advancement of Standards for Student Services/Development Programs.* Washington, D.C.: CAS, 1988.

Council on Postsecondary Accreditation (COPA). *The COPA Handbook.* Washington, D.C.: COPA, 1988.

International Association of Counseling Services (IACS). *Criteria and Standards for Accreditation of University and College Counseling Services.* Alexandria, Va.: IACS, 1982.

Kells, H. R. *Self-Study Processes: A Guide for Postsecondary Institutions.* New York: American Council on Education and Macmillan, 1983.

Lenn, M. P. "Accreditation, Certification, and Licensure." In M.A.F. Rehnke (ed.), *Creating Career Programs in a Liberal Arts Context.* New Directions for Higher Education, no. 57. San Francisco: Jossey-Bass, 1987.

Martin, W. B. *A College of Character: Renewing the Purpose and Content of College Education.* San Francisco: Jossey-Bass, 1982.

Miller, T. K., Thomas, W. L., Looney, S. C., and Yerian, J. *CAS Self Assessment Guides.* Washington, D.C.: Council for the Advancement of Standards for Student Services/Development Programs, 1988.

National Association for Foreign Student Affairs (NASFA). *NASFA Principles for International Educational Exchange.* Washington, D.C.: NASFA, 1981.

National Association of College and University Food Services (NACUFS). *The National Association of College and University Food Services Professional Standards Manual.* East Lansing, Mich.: NACUFS, 1982.

National Association of State Universities and Land Grant Colleges (NASULGC). *Statement of Principles on Student Outcomes Assessment.* Washington, D.C.: NASULGC, 1988.

National Intramural-Recreational Sports Association (NIRSA). *General and Specialty Standards for Collegiate Recreational Sports.* Corvallis, Oreg.: NIRSA, 1989.

Northwest Association of Schools and Colleges (NASC). *Standards.* Seattle, Wash.: NASC, 1988.

Southern Association of Colleges and Schools (SACS). *Criteria for Accreditation: Commission on Colleges.* Atlanta, Ga.: SACS, 1989–1990.

Phyllis Mable is vice-president for student affairs at Longwood College, Farmville, Virginia. She has served as president of the American College Personnel Association and is presently serving as president of the Council for the Advancement of Standards for Student Services/Development Programs. She is a recognized student development leader and specialist who has published extensively in the field of student affairs.

Professional standards are an important component of the process for accreditation of institutions and programs.

Professional Standards and the Accreditation Process

Barbara Jacoby, William L. Thomas, Jr.

The use and value of standards and interpretive guidelines as the bases of self-studies mandated by regional accrediting associations, as well as by student affairs associations (specialty areas), are examined in this chapter. Specific examples of the use of standards in the accreditation process and a review of potential issues and problems surrounding the use of standards as an accrediting tool in student affairs programs are also explored.

Purposes and Types of Accreditation

Accreditation is a system of assessing educational institutions and specialized programs affiliated with those institutions for a level of performance, integrity, and quality that entitles them to the confidence of the constituencies they serve. Unlike other countries where the federal governments regulate higher education, accreditation in the United States is performed by nongovernmental, voluntary professional associations. These groups establish standards for accreditation, arrange site visits, evaluate those institutions and programs that desire accredited status, and publicly recognize those in compliance with the established criteria. While accreditation is a voluntary process, its status forms the basis of many decisions by governmental funding agencies, scholarship boards, foundations, employees, and students that profoundly affect institutions and professional programs. The purposes of accreditation, as articulated by the Council on Postsecondary Accreditation ([COPA] 1989, p. 4), are as follows: "Foster excellence in postsecondary education through the development of criteria and guidelines for assessing educational effectiveness; encourage improvement through continuous self-study and review; assure the educational community, the general public, and other agencies or organizations that an institution or program has clearly defined and appropriate objectives, maintains conditions under which their achievement can reasonably be expected, is in fact accomplishing them substantially, and can be expected to continue to do so; provide counsel and assistance to established and developing institutions and programs; [and] endeavor to protect institutions against encroachments which jeopardize their educational effectiveness or academic freedom."

There are two types of accreditation in higher education. *Institutional accreditation* is granted by regional and national accrediting commissions and associations. These bodies accredit total operating units only. *Specialized accreditation* of professional and occupational schools and programs is granted by accrediting bodies established by national professional organizations in such fields as medicine, law, engineering, and counseling. All of these groups have established standards, or criteria, for accreditation.

For both institutional and specialized accreditation, the process begins with an institutional or program self-study. The self-study is a comprehensive assessment of how well the institution or program measures up to its previously established and stated goals and objectives. The resulting report serves as the basis for the site visit that is conducted by a visiting committee selected by the accrediting body. The site visit team usually consists of faculty, administrators, and appropriate specialists with expertise in the areas under consideration. The visitors review the self-study report and assess the institution or program in light of the findings in the report. Following the site visit, the committee prepares an evaluation report for the institution's review. The original self-study, the review team's report, and the response by the institution or program (if any) to that report are forwarded to the accreditation commission. A decision is then rendered regarding the institution's or program's accreditation status. Negative actions can be appealed according to procedures set out by each accrediting body.

Institutional Accreditation of Student Affairs

The six regional institutional accreditation bodies are the most significant for student affairs because they put forth standards for the philosophical basis and the practice of student affairs. There is a great range of philosophical orientations as well as operational specificity among the regional associations' standards (sometimes called criteria).

Philosophical statements regarding student development and student services are incorporated into most of the associations' standards. The Southern Association of Colleges and Schools ([SACS] 1989–1990, p. 33) has one of the strongest philosophical statements: "Student development services are essential to the achievement of the educational goals of the institution and should contribute to the cultural, social, moral, intellectual and physical development of students." The Northwest Association of Schools and Colleges ([NASC] 1988, p. 66) speaks directly of student welfare: "An institution should have and express a continuing concern for the total welfare of each student, including his/her physical and mental health, development of capabilities and talents, establishment of relationships with other persons, and motivation for progress in intellectual understanding." The philosophy of the Western Association of Schools and Colleges ([WASC] 1988, p. 67) is stated in terms of the institutional environment: "The institution supports a co-curricular environment that fosters the intellectual and personal development of students. That supportive environment is characterized by a concern for the welfare of all students, on and off campus."

The North Central Association of Colleges and Schools ([NCACS] 1988, p. 13), however, includes only the following lines regarding student services in one of its four general evaluative criteria: "Support programs, particularly those involving student services and learning resources, should receive careful attention. Residential campuses will differ markedly from commuter campuses. Research universities will have needs different from colleges." Carefully avoiding the assumption or statement that institutions are in the business of developing the whole person, the criterion indicates evaluative measures that should be implemented by "an institution concerned with student development apart from formal instruction" (NCACS, 1988, p. 14).

The regional associations' standards and guidelines for the administration of student services and student development programs vary as widely as their philosophical orientations. Nevertheless, most associations' statements include certain basic key elements.

One key element common to most accrediting associations' criteria is the establishment of goals or objectives for student services and student development programs. SACS (1989–1990, p. 33) includes in its criteria the statement that "goals for the student services program must be developed which are consistent with the student's needs and the purposes of the institution." Several associations ask that the objectives of the overall student affairs program and of the specific student services functions be set forth in the self-study completed prior to the accreditation site visit. Generally, the associations are interested in how student services' goals and objectives relate to the institution's mission and goals.

In addition to goals and objectives, the associations seek to learn through the accreditation process whether the administrative structure supporting the achievement of these goals is adequate. NASC (1988, p. 67), for example, seeks a detailed explanation of the organization for the "administration and coordination of the general student personnel program" together with an indication of "how faculty and student participation is provided for in the administration of the program." WASC (1988, p. 69) sets forth a specific standard for the coordination and administration of student services: "The institution has an administrative structure responsible for the overall coordination and administration of the co-curricular program. The institution provides staffing and resources commensurate with its level and size, with its goals for the co-curricular program, and with its institutional purposes."

SACS (1989–1990, p. 34) goes a step further by stating, "Student development services should be given organizational status commensurate with other major administrative areas within the institution." The Middle States Association of Colleges and Schools ([MSASC] 1987, p. 14) recognizes how administrative structures may vary among institutions: "Expressions of intent do not produce results; there must be definition, organization, and responsibility, although the forms may vary. Some institutions assign student personnel officers to a central staff; others prefer to diffuse them throughout the faculty. When the work enjoys good leadership and genuine faculty and staff support, the structure is less important than the results."

Regular evaluation of student services and student development programs is a concern reflected in many statements of standards. As one of its criterion statements, SACS (1989–1990, p. 34) maintains that "student development services and programs must be regularly evaluated." The New England Association of Schools and Colleges (1983, p. 47) asks directly, "What provisions are made for periodic evaluation of student personnel services? How recently has there been a structured evaluation?" Likewise, WASC specifies that students and faculty be involved in periodic program evaluation.

Regarding specific functional areas within student affairs, some associations merely list the individual student services that should be included in the institutional self-study. Others contain several pages setting forth specific standards for functional areas. By far the most comprehensive, NASC (1988) provides extensive guidelines for each student service, together with a description for the self-study of that service and specific questions for analysis and appraisal. SACS lists standards and guidelines for each program and service under its student development category. MSASC (1987) provides descriptive statements for several student services: retention, activities, athletics, placement and counseling, and records and data systems. Admissions is singled out by some associations for more elaborate standards and guidelines as well as for inclusion of analysis in the self-study.

As this volume goes to press, several regional accrediting associations are in the process of reviewing and revising their criteria for student affairs and other areas. Readers interested in obtaining the most current accreditation standards of particular regional associations should contact the office of their institution's chief executive officer or the appropriate regional institutional accrediting body. A list of accrediting agencies is located in Appendix A of this volume.

Specialized Accreditation of Student Affairs Functions

Few of the nearly fifty programs that are subject to COPA's specialized accreditation are of direct interest to college and university student affairs administrators. These include student affairs, counseling, and counseling psychology preparation programs. In addition, several non-COPA agencies are involved in accrediting college and university health services and counseling and testing centers.

Two associations (Accreditation Association for Ambulatory Health Care and Joint Commission on Accreditation of Healthcare Organizations) accredit college and university health centers using established standards for ambulatory health care, including such outpatient settings as health maintenance organizations, ambulatory surgery centers, birthing centers, and college health centers. The American College Health Association also publishes standards for college health programs but performs no accreditation functions. Standards for college health programs require the same level of quality as those for other public and private medical institutions. For most programs, one or two years of preparation are required to ensure that the criteria for accreditation can be met. The health care standards are also useful in the creation or development of campus health programs.

Academic programs of professional preparation can also be accredited. Programs that prepare student affairs practitioners and community, mental health, and school counselors at the master's degree level, as well as doctoral programs in counselor education, may be accredited by the Council for Accreditation of Counseling and Related Educational Programs (1988), the accrediting arm of the American Association for Counseling and Development. The American Psychological Association (APA) accredits doctoral training programs in counseling psychology and internships in professional psychology. College counseling centers, to be eligible to serve as counseling psychology internship sites must also be accredited by the APA. The International Association of Counseling Services also functions as an accrediting agency for college and university counseling centers. Although other standards, guidelines, and principles of professional practice have been developed by professional organizations such as the Council for the Advancement of Standards for Student Services/Development Programs (CAS), the National Association of Foreign Student Affairs, and the American Association of College Registrars and Admission Officers, accreditation is limited largely to the agencies previously identified. Further information about those specialized accrediting bodies can be obtained directly from the agencies listed in Appendix B.

Issues Related to the Use of Standards in the Accreditation of Student Affairs Functions

Several issues regarding the use of standards in the accreditation of student affairs functions deserve our attention. Some of these are controversial, and an attempt is made here to represent various views.

Effectiveness of Regional Associations' Standards. To gather qualitative, anecdotal information regarding the current use of standards in accreditation of student affairs and related issues, we conducted an informal telephone survey of student affairs professionals who have had significant involvement in the accreditation process. The survey respondents generally agreed that the various accrediting agencies' standards are vague in the area of student affairs, with some feeling that the general nature of the standards is necessitated by the wide diversity of institutions to which they must apply and that the standards provide sufficient guidance to visiting accrediting committees. But some respondents felt that the current standards were at best minimally effective and did not seriously challenge institutions to improve their student service programs.

Respondents favored the maintenance of regional associations' standards as the bases of accreditation of student affairs programs rather than nationally established standards such as those of CAS. Several individuals believed that the CAS standards should be used by student affairs practitioners in preparing the self-studies required for accreditation purposes. In addition, they felt that the CAS standards should be used by the accrediting team members in assessing student services and when making recommendations as part of the report following site visits. Several respondents hoped that regional accrediting associations would use the CAS standards as guides when revising their own standards so as to make them more thorough and specific.

Accountability. Proponents of concrete, well-defined standards believe that the use of standards and guidelines promotes institutions' accountability. Standards can be used by student affairs practitioners to communicate more precisely to students, for example, what they can and should expect in the way of services, programs, and individual assistance. Too few students know to ask, "Exactly what can you (the practitioner, the program, the institution) do for me?" Likewise, too few agencies are required to provide a prescribed series of actions, activities, and programs at a specified level of quality.

Those who discourage the use of uniform standards (other than extremely vague and general statements) may fear that such standards formally embraced by the institution could be viewed as *contracts* that will make the institution, in some new, more burdensome ways, legally liable for the effective delivery of services and programs. However, higher education need not guarantee that its services and programs are effective in their outcomes for individual students, and undue legal liability is unlikely to result from the establishment of reasonable standards.

Enhancement of Understanding of the Student Affairs Profession. The development of standards for student affairs has gone a long way in expressing what the complex profession is about. Because the heart of student affairs work is facilitating the development of students in an almost limitless number and kind of ways, it has been exceedingly difficult for the profession to communicate effectively the nature of its work. Thus, student affairs work has been neither widely understood nor well appreciated by students, faculty, and other administrators. Over the years student affairs has too often been seen as supportive and secondary, rather than integral, to institutions' main missions. If clearly articulated standards were established, the profession would benefit greatly from the broader understanding and confidence that are likely to result among faculty and administrative colleagues.

Student affairs standards can also help presidents and other institutional leaders communicate better the institutions' goals and aspirations to supporting constituencies. The president will be able to establish campus priorities with a greater sense of how human development concerns interact with academic, financial, physical, and political concerns.

In his introduction to *CAS Standards and Guidelines* (CAS, 1986, p. vii), James Vickery, president of the University of Montevallo and a charter member of the Advisory Committee on Self-Regulation Initiatives of the American Council on Education, provided extraordinary support for the idea of professional standards for student affairs: "As a college president, I am indebted to CAS for thus providing me so unusual a statement of specific program missions and so useful a framework for campus evaluation. I am confident that when this book of standards and guidelines has been widely distributed by ACT [American College Testing Program] my colleagues on other campuses will feel the same way, even if they happen to disagree with the particulars of any of them. Who knows? Thereby might *all* college and university presidents come to appreciate even more than many of them now do the 'extras' inherent in the cocurricular activities of student services/student development personnel!"

There are other constituencies of importance, including parents, local and national legislators, the media, high school counselors, alumni, and potential employers of students. Almost anyone with an interest in or connection with the institution will be better served by knowing and understanding more precisely what student affairs agencies do and are designed to accomplish.

Inclusion of Student Affairs in Institutional Self-Studies. Institutions have great latitude in selecting the aspects of institutional life that they desire to include in the accreditation self-study. Historically, some institutions have omitted student affairs services and programs from self-studies for a variety of reasons. In some instances, nonacademic student services have not been clearly defined or organized. Or, it has been feared that student affairs functions have no accountability criteria by which their outcomes could be measured within the scope of an institutional self-study. In other cases, student affairs staff members have not earned enough credits within their institutions to provide the political clout required to succeed in establishing student affairs as a priority for self-study. This reality is related to the general lack of understanding from which the profession has suffered on the national level. The very existence of *CAS Standards and Guidelines* for the various functional areas of student affairs practice enhances the likelihood of the inclusion of those areas in future accreditation self-studies.

One viable approach to enhancing the role and function of student services and student development programs in relation to accreditation self-studies is to involve outside consultants in the process. Inviting a recognized expert in the area of student affairs or specific functional areas to campus to review the program(s) not only has great utility for increasing the likelihood that the self-study will be well executed but also provides a staff development opportunity. If quality programs are sought, it is often helpful to invite individuals with high levels of expertise to campus as a means for stimulating the self-study process.

Involvement of Student Affairs Expertise in Regional Accreditation. Because student affairs functions have not consistently been included in accreditation self-studies, site visit teams selected by accrediting associations have often not included members with expertise in the evaluation of student services and student affairs programs. Consequently, faculty members or administrators with little experience in student affairs practice would then be asked, "By the way, would you please take a look at the student life arena?", usually coupled with assignments in their own areas of expertise. It is not difficult to imagine the low-quality evaluations that such an approach encourages. But it is difficult to imagine a visiting student affairs administrator being asked to review one or more of the institution's educational programs if time allowed. Higher education cannot afford for either the curricular or the cocurricular aspects to be short-circuited in the accreditation self-study process. Both are essential and deserve relatively equal attention.

It is also true that some accreditation committee visitors who hold positions in student affairs at one type of institution may be only marginally qualified to evaluate the effectiveness of student services and programs on another type of campus. Such an event may occur if the accrediting association selects a student affairs practitioner who does not have sufficient breadth and depth of knowledge to evaluate another program objectively with the limited standards provided. In addition, the training of visiting team members varies widely in thoroughness. When the expertise of the evaluators of student affairs programs is at a less than optimum level, it is likely that the review will be low quality and relatively useless. Although *CAS Standards and Guidelines* is an effective tool for site team members to supplement their experience and working knowledge of student services, it is imperative that only the most credible practitioners be invited to participate in the important accreditation review and evaluation process.

Conclusion

Professional standards established at both the regional and national levels have utility for the accreditation process. The use of such standards in institutional self-studies and in reports submitted by accreditation site visit teams significantly contributes to the credibility and utility of the evaluations. It is through quality evaluative efforts that student services and programs improve and that the image of the profession is enhanced.

In order for improvements to be achieved, however, all concerned with student affairs programs must strive for quality assurance in their professional activities. Regular and systematic self-studies are essential to quality performance. When the institution's decennial accreditation reaffirmation self-study is being planned, student affairs practitioners should be intimately involved in the process and procedures required to bring it about. In-depth program, staff, and student outcome evaluations are needed to go well beyond the mere academic exercise that institutional self-study represents when done for no other reason than to ensure compliance with minimal accreditation standards.

Professional standards that transcend those of the accrediting agencies have special utility for quality assurance. Use of the CAS standards and self-assessment guides (CAS, 1986, 1988), for instance, provides most programs with ample data for accreditation purposes. The inclusion of outside consultants in the early phases of the accreditation self-study process is especially valuable, for such individuals can provide a fresh, objective perspective to the whole process that will not otherwise be available. Although the accreditation process is designed to assess how well an institution and its programs are in compliance with a specified set of minimal standards, the related self-study process is highly useful for strategic and long-range planning purposes as well. To do less than the best one can do is perhaps easier, but it lacks an element of professionalism that is essential to the future of an important student development enterprise.

References

Council for the Accreditation of Counseling and Related Educational Programs (CACREP). *Accreditation Procedures Manual and Application.* Alexandria, Va.: CACREP, 1988.

Council for the Advancement of Standards for Student Services/Development Programs (CAS). *CAS Standards and Guidelines for Student Services/Development Programs.* Washington, D.C.: CAS, 1986.

Council for the Advancement of Standards for Student Services/Development Programs. *CAS Self Assessment Guides.* Washington, D.C.: CAS, 1988.

Council on Postsecondary Accreditation (COPA). *The COPA Handbook.* Washington, D.C.: COPA, 1989.

Keesee, G. S. "Directory of Accredited Programs." *CACREP Connection Newsletter,* 1989, *1,* 9.

Middle States Association of Colleges and Schools (MSACS). Commission on Higher Education. *Characteristics of Excellence in Higher Education.* Philadelphia: MSACS, 1987.

New England Association of Schools and Colleges, Inc. (NEASC). Commission on Institutions of Higher Education. *Accreditation Handbook.* Winchester, Mass.: NEASC, 1983.

North Central Association of Colleges and Schools (NCACS). Commission on Institutions of Higher Education. *A Guide to Self-Study for Commission Evaluation.* Chicago: NCACS, 1988.

Northwest Association of Schools and Colleges (NASC). *Standards.* Seattle, Wash.: NASC, 1988.

Southern Association of Colleges and Schools (SACS). Commission on Colleges. *Criteria for Accreditation: Commission on Colleges.* Atlanta, Ga.: SACS, 1989–1990.

Western Association of Schools and Colleges (WASC). Accrediting Commission for Senior Colleges and Universities. *Handbook of Accreditation.* Oakland, Calif.: WASC, 1988.

Barbara Jacoby is director of the Office of Commuter Affairs at the University of Maryland, College Park. She also serves as director of the National Clearinghouse for Commuter Programs and as a member of the CAS Board of Directors.

William L. Thomas, Jr., is vice-president for student affairs at the University of Maryland, College Park. He has served as National Association of Student Personnel Administrators representative to and secretary of CAS since its establishment in 1979.

Various approaches can be used to put standards into practice for program evaluation and planning within a division of student affairs.

Operationalizing CAS Standards for Program Evaluation and Planning

William A. Bryan, Richard H. Mullendore

In Spring 1986, the American College Testing Program, on behalf of the Council for the Advancement of Standards for Student Services/Development Programs (CAS), distributed copies of *CAS Standards and Guidelines* to every chief executive officer of an institution of higher education in the United States. In the foreword for CAS (1986, p. vii) President James Vickery stated, "CAS has moved ahead commendably . . . to set forth standards and guidelines for professional practice. In doing so, CAS not only has established the 'student affairs' profession as a leader in the self-regulation movement, but also has encouraged other higher education organizations to go and do likewise." Twenty-two CAS member organizations were responsible for the CAS publication, which outlined sixteen functional area standards and guidelines for student affairs programs. With the publication of this historic document and the involvement of so many professional associations in its creation, the student affairs profession clearly announced its determination to control its own destiny by establishing "criteria to guide the professional practice in preparation of student services, student affairs, and student development program personnel in post-secondary institutions of higher learning" (CAS, 1986, p. ix). These standards constitute an evolving document, one that can be changed periodically to be current with criteria for functional areas in student affairs. From the upper ranks of the chief executive officer and the chief student affairs officer on down the administrative hierarchy, a challenge is presented to those who work in the student affairs profession on a daily basis: effectively apply and operationalize these standards in the collegiate setting.

This chapter highlights the importance of incorporating and operationalizing CAS standards and guidelines within institutions for the self-assessment, evaluation, and short- and long-range planning of programs. We provide a rationale for applying these standards within a division of student affairs and discuss approaches for using the standards in functional areas of the division. We also provide a strategy for an annual review of functional areas, involving an assessment of components such as mission, program, and human resources and an evaluation of progress toward meeting or going beyond the minimal standards. In short, our central theme is that for a division of student affairs to be a dynamic, effective organization, it must not only establish quality professional practice in the here and now but also anticipate student needs and plan accordingly for the future.

Operationalizing CAS Standards and Guidelines for Self-Assessment and Evaluation

The development of the CAS standards represents one of the greatest achievements of our profession. These materials represent an excellent set of tools to develop, expand, explain, and defend important campus services. Yet, five years after distribution to every college and university in the country, only a handful of institutions have actually developed and implemented a process for operationalizing these standards. In light of this discouraging information and in an effort to motivate the profession, it is helpful to (1) examine some of the reasons why it is important to put the CAS standards to use in all institutions and (2) provide sample approaches to operationalizing the standards within functional areas.

Rationale for Operationalization. Miller and Prince (1976) wrote that student affairs programs and professionals have been very helpful to students, but that many faculty and students view these programs as merely complementary or supplementary to classroom teaching. They argued that "the full potential of students will not be developed until the emotional and physical aspects of their growth are given as much attention as the cognitive dimension. The informal curriculum of student affairs programs deserves coordinate status with formal instruction" (1976, p. 2). Now, fifteen years later, the profession of student affairs is still seeking this status.

Equal status will not be accorded on many campuses until the student affairs staff can appropriately document the value of its many functions and educate others within the institution regarding that value. "Forward thinking institutions should begin the assessment process in student affairs before it is thrust upon them from the outside [if this has not already happened]. Progressive divisions of student affairs may be able to influence future directions and uses of assessment in their areas only if they have an ongoing assessment program in place" (Erwin, 1989, p. 586).

There are many reasons why staff should aggressively pursue operationalization of the CAS standards. According to the CAS Executive Committee (CAS, 1986, p. ix), "Whether for purposes of program development, accreditation self-study, staff development, program evaluation, or making comparisons across institutions, these standards and guidelines represent the most current thinking and considered judgment of those primarily responsible for the cocurricular life and educational experiences of college students." Some discussion regarding these purposes and others may be helpful to colleagues who are seeking the motivation to begin to put CAS standards to use in their particular institutional settings.

Program Development. As divisions of student affairs assess the needs of and changes within their particular student populations, new programs frequently are developed or enhanced. CAS standards and guidelines can provide an excellent blueprint for program establishment or enhancement.

Accreditation Self-Study. Some accrediting associations have "implemented new criteria for reaffirmation that include both a statement of specific educational goals and documentation of how well students are meeting those goals. In most cases, institutions have the flexibility to determine their own educational objectives and assessment methods but must provide evidence of program quality" (Erwin, 1989, p. 585). One way to accomplish this quality assurance is to provide evidence of compliance with professional standards and guidelines established outside the institution.

Staff Development. Engaging in the processes of self-assessment and evaluation can be a powerful staff development tool, especially if staff are involved in the assessment of functional areas other than their own.

Program Evaluation. Operationalization of CAS standards and guidelines provides a comprehensive and consistent framework for program evaluation.

Comparisons Across Institutions. Student affairs staff members are often concerned with program quality, funding, and components relative to programs of colleagues at similar institutions. Utilization of CAS standards and guidelines provides the opportunity for staff to appropriately compare programs due to consistency of language and format.

Development/Enhancement of Program Credibility. The CAS standards and guidelines can be very helpful in reducing the *credibility gap* between the student affairs staff and other constituencies. For example, knowing that the standards exist and knowing that the campus judicial system is in compliance with those standards may provide encouragement to the faculty to refer cases of academic dishonesty rather than try to handle them ad hoc within an academic department.

Institutional Acceptance of Programs/Departments. Scott (1978, pp. 30–31) wrote that "student support services are one of the first areas to be cut in retrenchment because there appears to be an endless need for them, there are conflicts of opinion about who should pay for them, there is no way of telling when enough are offered, there are no objective methods to evaluate whether or not they are successful, and there is no compelling argument that these services must be provided by specialists." Use of CAS standards and guidelines can help in addressing all of Scott's concerns.

Education of the Campus Community. As a department begins the process of operationalizing the standards and guidelines, it is recommended that faculty, staff, and students be asked to collaboratively participate in the self-assessment and evaluation of each functional area. This process will likely serve as an educational experience for those who are involved.

Improved Political Maneuverability. Student affairs staff members often seek appropriate political leverage within their institutions in order to accomplish program objectives. The need to comply with minimal national standards is easily understood and accepted as a rationale for institutional/political change because of the already established precedent in academic departments.

Budgetary Assistance. Competition for dollars within a department, division, or institution is often fierce. As with political maneuverability, the need to comply with standards can be very helpful in making a case for additional program financial support.

Many other reasons can be cited for a division of student affairs to operationalize the CAS standards and guidelines. One crucial question to ask is why not put the standards into operation? The next section provides information regarding involvement in the assessment process and approaches for conducting a functional area self-assessment and evaluation.

Approaches to Operationalization. Once the motivation exists for applying the CAS standards and guidelines to ongoing practice, it is important to look at the process of functional area self-assessment and evaluation. There are a variety of methods that can be employed, and chief student affairs officers should consider using a process that will maximize the visibility and credibility of the self-assessment and evaluation effort.

It is recommended that each functional area review be conducted by a group that includes faculty, staff (student affairs and others), and students, as well as the person primarily responsible for the program. In some cases, it may be appropriate to involve alumni, persons from the community, and members of the Board of Trustees. This involvement in the operationalization process is important for several reasons. First, by involving people other than those with direct responsibility for program implementation, there will likely be greater objectivity exhibited. An orientation director may be too close to the program to assess and evaluate some program components objectively. Second, involvement is an excellent staff development tool for student affairs staff who assist in a review of a functional area other than their own. The process helps staff to better understand how other programs and departments operate. Third, involvement of students is important because they are the constituency being served. Their assessment of student services is extremely important. Fourth, involvement of faculty members and others inside or outside the institution serves as a tremendous educational opportunity for student affairs professionals, an opportunity to let other constituencies know that standards exist and that it is important to comply with, if not exceed, minimal national standards. This involvement provides an opportunity to educate, to increase credibility, to gain greater acceptance, and even to increase institutional support for programs. If a division of student affairs involves three faculty members in the assessment of each of nineteen functional areas, then over fifty faculty members can potentially become allies of, if not advocates for, student affairs programs.

In some settings, it may be appropriate and important to utilize the services of an external consultant to facilitate the process of operationalizing standards. A consultant can provide a level of objectivity and expertise that is helpful in moving the process forward.

Consider now the following two sample approaches to the operationalization of CAS standards and guidelines within functional areas.

Approach 1: Use of the CAS Self-Assessment Guides. In 1988, CAS published self-assessment guides for sixteen functional areas within student affairs. These guides are designed to help an institution "gain an informed perspective on its strengths and deficiencies and then plan for program improvement" (CAS, 1988, p. iii). Each self-assessment guide is divided into three sections. The first section provides an introduction to the CAS standards and guidelines, explains the self-assessment process, and describes the steps necessary for the development of a follow-up action plan. The second section of the guide provides worksheets for the assessment of the thirteen component parts of each functional area. The worksheets include the following: (1) assessment criteria for determining the extent to which the program is in compliance with the standards, (2) space for including selected CAS guidelines as additional assessment criteria for the self-study, (3) a scale for rating compliance judgments, (4) space for identifying and summarizing evaluation evidence (documentation), (5) space for describing discrepancies between assessment criteria and actual program practice, (6) space for delineating required corrective actions that need to be taken, and (7) space for recommending special actions for program enhancement (CAS, 1988, p. iii). The third section of the guide provides a copy of the standards and guidelines for the functional area.

The self-assessment guides can be purchased from CAS and reproduced by an institution for self-study purposes. The guides focus specifically on each CAS statement of standards. Special effort and interpretation are necessary to use the guides for assessment of the CAS standards (*must* statements). These guides are designed to be completed by individual staff members, independently of other potential raters. CAS recommends that if more than one person is going to complete the ratings, then training for raters should be provided. Difference in perceptions can later be identified and "a group consensus can be sought" (CAS, 1988, p. iv).

Program self-assessment and evaluation using the guides rely heavily on documentation. "The collection, documentation, and inclusion of supporting evidence is an essential first step in the assessment process" (CAS, 1988, p. iii). Therefore, each rater must have access to program publications, surveys, evaluation data, résumés, job descriptions, budgets, and other documents.

A key component of the self-assessment guides is the recommendation that a follow-up action plan be developed. "This plan identifies future directions on the basis of comparing past performance with desired outcomes" (CAS, 1988, p. v). This plan should include areas of excellence, required actions, program enhancement actions, and program action plans.

Approach 2: Development of Program Statements and Recommendations. The CAS standards and guidelines were available in draft form in 1985, in final form in 1986, and or some functional areas in 1987 and later. The CAS self-assessment guides were first published in 1988. In 1986 at the University of North Carolina at Wilmington (UNCW), between the times the standards and the self-assessment guides were published, an approach was developed for operationalizing the orientation standards and guidelines. This approach was developed because there was a tremendous immediate need for campus-wide education, credibility, and political maneuverability within the new-student orientation program. The approach was so successful that it was refined and applied throughout all functional areas under the control of the student affairs division.

The program statement approach relies greatly on group process. The program director for each functional area is responsible for locating or creating an appropriate group to work on the standards. This group may be an existing advisory board or standing committee, or it may be a special task force or ad hoc committee created specifically for the purpose of assessing the functional area. The program director must ensure that the group identified or created includes representatives from all appropriate constituencies. There is no formula for the size of the group, in that the needs of various functional areas are quite different. For example, because the student orientation program involves most campus facilities and staff and faculty members from several areas, that committee may need to be larger than others if all appropriate constituencies are to be involved in the self-assessment process.

The chairperson of the board, committee, or task force should be carefully selected. This person may or may not be the person administratively responsible for the functional area. This person must, however, be knowledgeable about the functional area, committed to the self-assessment process, and able to keep the group on task throughout the process.

Because group process is the key element in the program statement approach, it is suggested that a set of goals for the process be developed that dictate the agenda for the group meetings. These goals should include the following: (1) to brief the group on the background of CAS and to distribute copies of the CAS general standards and the CAS standards and guidelines for the functional area; (2) to provide an opportunity to discuss the material included in the CAS documents; (3) to understand, discuss, and assess the general standards; (4) to understand, discuss, and assess each of the nine component parts of the functional area standards and guidelines; (5) to develop accurate and appropriate program statements that reflect the existing status of each component of the functional area relative to both the standards and the guidelines; (6) to identify problems, weaknesses, and areas of noncompliance, and to develop appropriate recommendations to address these areas; (7) to identify areas in which the functional area needs to move beyond the standards and guidelines, and to make appropriate recommendations; (8) to accept the CAS standards and guidelines, program statements, and recommendations as appropriate working documents for the functional area; (9) to establish a process of annual review of the program statements and recommendations; and (10) to develop a report regarding the process, results, and recommendations, and to distribute it as appropriate throughout and beyond the institution.

In the program statement approach, the group arrives at consensus on the material to be submitted. It is important that the program director for each functional area submit the final report utilizing a standard format, since this approach does not use the standardized forms included in the self-assessment guides. The decision regarding the type of consistent format rests with the chief student affairs officer.

Approach 1 Versus Approach 2. Before comparing and contrasting the two approaches, it should be noted that there are, no doubt, other approaches that institutions may employ to put the standards into place. It is imperative, however, that institutions develop an appropriate mechanism to study and adopt the CAS standards and guidelines.

Both of the approaches described here have several similarities. Each requires some person(s) within the institution to have or develop extensive knowledge of the CAS standards and guidelines and the various functional areas. Both approaches require considerable documentation of the existing program in preparation for the process of self-assessment. Both approaches may provide useful working documents that can be reviewed on an annual basis. And, most important, both approaches require the development of specific recommendations for program improvement.

By contrast, use of the self-assessment guides relies primarily on independent individual ratings, while the program statement approach focuses on group discussion throughout the assessment process. The guides are extremely structured and detailed, while the program statements lack some of the depth of the guides. The program statement approach provides a relatively comprehensive program overview, while the guides demand a full program self-study. Finally, the guides focus on the actual standards statements (compliance with what must be), while the program statements examine the standards and guidelines as a total package (of what is and should be).

As a department or division develops an approach appropriate to the setting, a combination of these two approaches may be beneficial. For example, the group process emphasis on approach 2 may be combined with the full self-study components of approach 1 to provide both an excellent educational opportunity for staff and others and a structured, in-depth rating process for the functional area.

Annual Review (Evaluation) of Standards and Guidelines. When CAS was formed, three goals were developed and pursued. "The first was to establish, adopt and disseminate two types of standards and guidelines. . . . The second goal was to assist professionals and institutions in the utilization and implementation of these standards and guidelines. . . . Third, CAS strove to establish a system of regular evaluation of standards and guidelines" (CAS, 1986, p. 1). These goals can also be operationalized at the institutional level. The first two have already been addressed in this chapter. The third goal addresses the issue of ongoing evaluation, which is critical to the long-term value of the standards and guidelines. Once a functional area self-assessment has been completed, it is important that the documents remain visible. This requires periodic reassessment; and it is recommended that the evaluation occur annually and that it be integrated with a departmental annual report, because this integration requires that functional area staffs review the CAS materials annually yet does not require a tremendous separate time commitment. A relatively simple three-step process is suggested in order to complete the annual review (evaluation) for each functional area.

First, the program director should review the existing program statements or self-assessment materials. This review may occur with the group that developed the initial materials. Recommendations for revisions should be developed and submitted to the chief student affairs officer. Second, discussions of the suggested revisions should occur between the program director and the chief student affairs officer. Third, agreed-upon revisions should be made and included as a part of the annual report. Special needs should be highlighted. The next section takes this process several steps forward by describing how the CAS materials can be integrated into program planning.

Operationalizing CAS Standards and Guidelines for Program Planning

For a division of student affairs to anticipate student needs before problems occur, proper planning is needed. Professional staff must anticipate and identify basic activities and programs necessary to respond to student needs in each student affairs department and set priorities within the various work settings. Information gained from a needs assessment may lead to the identification of necessary staffing and other resources as educators seek to properly serve students.

Description/Definition of Planning Within Student Affairs. Planning is a process that involves most student affairs professionals on a daily basis. Information and knowledge gained through planning help student affairs professionals to determine needs for staffing and other resources. No task in student affairs is less attended to than planning. Yet, if student affairs professionals do not plan for their own future, someone else will. Planning entails clear statements about expected results as well as about functions considered essential to the operation of each department within the division. If leaders are appropriately prepared in divisions of student affairs, they will have the information needed when asked, "Who do you serve? What is your client load? How many contacts did you have with students in the past year? Why do students drop out? What are the needs of students? What are the major concerns of the students on campus today?"

Overview of Common Planning Models. Styles (1985) summarized and reviewed the strengths of a number of program-planning models in student affairs, including those of Kaiser (1972), Drum and Figler (1973), Lewis and Lewis (1974), Aulepp and Delworth (1976), Morrill, Oetting, and Hurst (1974), Moore and Delworth (1976), and Miller and Prince (1976). Some of these models focus on specific functional areas in student affairs. As apparent from a review of the literature, there are numerous planning models for institutions of higher education. Cope (1987, p. 98) outlined what he termed "six quasi-models or approaches to planning." He summarized the formal-rational, organizational development, technocratic/empirical, philosophical synthesis, political advocacy, and coordinated anarchy models. Foxley (1980) presented a number of popular management (planning) models for the consideration of student affairs staff: Planning Program and Budgeting Systems (PPBS), Management Information Systems (MIS), Organizational Development (OD), and Management by Objectives (MBO).

Clearly, the planning model selected for use must be adapted to the needs of each local setting. Therefore, it is probably wise that each student affairs division adapt from existing models or develop anew a planning model that meets its own unique needs.

What Is Planning and Why Is It Important? Most student affairs professionals view planning as involving the following major elements: identification of a need or problem, assessment of constraints, goal statements, objectives, activities, program structure, budgeting, and evaluation (Harpel, 1980). Clearly, in the planning process within a division of student affairs, it is extremely important that all players follow a similar course of action in carrying out a division mission. Common terminology and meanings are extremely important. The involvement of all staff in the exploration of ideas is also important. Each staff member within a department should understand the importance of his or her role in the accomplishment of a department mission, as well as the basic goals of the division. Planning involves "a conscious choice of ideas, goals, objectives, program structure, and action patterns designed to coordinate efforts of people for some period of time toward chosen broad goals" (Tincher, 1983, p. 436). Planning, typically, is long range (beyond five years) or short range (from six months to five years). The process of planning is important to student affairs practitioners in that they can gain a sense of direction and purpose, evaluate feedback, identify unmet needs of students, as well as of staff, and gain the necessary resources to carry out their assigned responsibilities. A good planning model may bring external recognition and visibility to a division of student affairs. As Harpel (1980, p. 298) has suggested, "improved student affairs management programs will have a positive effect upon the delivery of services, staff morale, and upon the political milieu as well."

Rationale for Integrating CAS Standards and Guidelines into Planning Materials. With the development of standards for student services by CAS, there is now a statement of minimum, essential elements expected of any institution conducting student services/development programs in higher education. The standards and guidelines outlined in this document give direct guidance to the campus student affairs program as it seeks to develop student services/development programs that meet the needs of students on the college campus. Each campus can now evaluate its student affairs functional areas against the minimum requirements of CAS. If campuses find there are special unmet needs in the program, human resources, or one of the other components, correction of these deficiencies can become part of the planning process to bring the program into compliance with CAS standards.

By integrating CAS standards into a student affairs planning process, each functional area can determine future (or annual) objectives that relate to each component within the functional area standard. This assessment allows a division of student affairs to move beyond minimal compliance. Annual program objectives may necessitate budget development or special resources for implementation. Justification for budget requests, or other resources, is readily available in each standards statement, since it is accepted as a national guide supported by the student affairs profession. Goals and objectives that come out of a review of each functional area can quickly provide impetus for needed change in program areas of student affairs. For this process to be maximally beneficial, it is important to include faculty, students, and other constituents beyond the division of student affairs.

By integrating CAS standards and guidelines into the planning materials of a division of student affairs, any objective in a functional area can be easily categorized into one of the nine CAS components: mission, program, organization and administration, human resources, funding, facilities, campus and community relations, ethics, or evaluation. For example, in a university union there may be a planning objective that, under the category of human resources, calls for an increase of professional staff to respond to student recreational requirements. This planning objective potentially touches the funding, facility development, and evaluation components of CAS standards. By meeting the staffing requirements for recreational programs, there is compliance with the human resources section of the Standards and Guidelines for College Unions in the *CAS Standards and Guidelines.* CAS standards are useful in a division's planning process as they provide a vehicle for easily justifying stated needs. This document can be a powerful impetus for needed change in a specific functional area.

A Case Application: Integrating CAS Standards and Guidelines into Program Planning Materials

In this section, the planning process at UNCW is presented as an example. For several years at UNCW, CAS standards have been an important part of the planning process in the division of student affairs. In 1986, small review teams of students, faculty, and staff were organized for most functional areas. These review teams made recommendations that assisted the process of bringing functional areas into compliance with the minimum standards outlined by CAS or that allowed program areas to go beyond these minimum standards. Recommendations were reviewed by each department and then forwarded to the vice-chancellor for student affairs; in some cases, specific recommendations were discussed with the chancellor.

For each functional area, the team reviewed where the particular program presently was and made specific recommendations regarding the nine CAS components. The teams referred to the general CAS standards during this review process for additional information as they made recommendations. In essence, they developed mission and program statements for each functional area, outlining what currently existed, updated organizational charts, and stated policies for functional areas. They also outlined human resources in departmental work areas, identified funding available to carry out commitments, identified facilities available (square footage, office sizes, and so on), assessed compliance with ethics statements, and identified evaluation processes. Since 1986, functional area statements have been reviewed annually. Originally, the CAS review process involved two parts: (1) review of CAS standards and guidelines and development of program statements for sixteen functional areas and (2) formulation of recommendations to assist functional areas in changing programs to meet or exceed stated standards.

The annual planning model of the UNCW Division of Student Affairs consists of four parts. Part One is the development of a mission statement;

Part Two is the development of key program results; Part Three is the identification of problem-solving objectives; and Part Four is the development of innovative goals for the future (one year or longer). This planning model is adapted from Deegan and Fritz (1975). Division worksheets for key program results, problem-solving objectives, and innovative goals are adapted from this publication as well. Key program results are composed of the major component parts of a job in each functional area. These component parts may come from the mission statement or from a program statement and should reflect the major responsibilities within each functional area. Problem-solving objectives are established for each functional area by identifying program results that are considered below acceptable standards. Innovative goals are determined from needed changes, desired programs or activities, or new directions or special needs within a particular functional area. On this worksheet, each department seeks to bring about some new contribution to its mission or program. In each planning section for the Division of Student Affairs at UNCW, component parts of functional areas may be included. For example, within the college union functional area, key program results for the union may be leisure time and recreational opportunities. Under a problem-solving objective, a union might indicate dissatisfaction with its organizational chart or administrative structure and desire to make changes, or it might indicate dissatisfaction with facilities for its recreation programs. As an innovative goal, a union might develop a plan over a five-year period to create a new union program in recreation activities or else develop an addition to an existing union to meet specific program needs.

Strategies for Using CAS Standards and Guidelines for Short- and Long-Term Planning. Outlined in the previous section is the process that is used at UNCW for short-term planning. The innovative goal statements that are developed on an annual basis can actually apply for one year or longer and in essence may be a part of the long-term planning process. On the long-range planning worksheets (five-year planning periods) departments are asked to identify ideas for implementation (that is, mission, program, human resources, organization and administration, and so on). Functional areas then identify the assumptions or needs underlying these ideas and formulate methods for implementing the goal statements with respect to costs, time frames, and expected results.

This method has complemented the student affairs role in the university's long-range planning process. In this process, either the chief student affairs officer or department directors have the opportunity to present information from the worksheets to a university planning committee and to clarify stated goals. By 1988, the Division of Student Affairs was able to present to the UNCW University Planning Committee a document outlining standards statements that followed the CAS format for every functional area within student affairs.

Process of Annual Review of CAS Standards and Guidelines Relative to Program Planning. On an annual basis, the standards statements developed by functional areas in the Division of Student Affairs are revised according to problems or needs of goal implementation encountered during the year. For example, again in the university union, changes in staffing pattern or in facilities available to a program might be required to achieve the annual goals. The changes within the division standards statements are reflected by functional areas as of June 30 of each year.

As a part of each department's annual report, there is a CAS statement update. Part One of the report highlights departmental program changes that have occurred during the year. In Part Two, the key program results worksheets are completed with level of attainment of stated goals, as well as a summary of the status of problem-solving objectives. Within this section, there is also a brief summary of the status of each innovative goal. In Part Three, organization and administration, there is a review of the organizational structure of the department and of the changes that have occurred, as well as a narrative describing other departmental highlights. Changes in governance or programming structures, for example, can be included in this section for each functional area. In Part Four, human resources, there is a listing of staff, staff changes, resignations, and retirements. In Part Five, campus and community relations, each department outlines campus and community outreach, and professional development activities for staff and programs. Additional involvement of new constituencies is also outlined in this section. Part Six, ethics and evaluation, includes any changes that are included in a program's ethical statement, and a departmental summary of efforts to meet annual evaluation goals. Also, evaluation processes for providing feedback from users of services as well as special research projects undertaken within a department are highlighted in this section of the annual report.

Summary

For the past several years at UNCW, *CAS Standards and Guidelines* (CAS, 1986) has provided a basis for self-study. In this process, the Division of Student Affairs has had the opportunity to review goals of functional areas and the status of program development and new desired outcomes. These national standards have assisted departments in accomplishing needed changes and have provided a basis for justifying proposed changes. As the campus looks forward to a reaccreditation visit, staff members believe the process followed over the past five years has placed the division in a solid position to respond efficiently to any special requests from a reaccreditation visit team.

The CAS standards and guidelines have been educational tools used by staff to educate faculty, other administrative staff members, Board of Trustee members, and students. Education has occurred as a result of these constituencies being actively involved in a review process of functional program areas in the division. Increased numbers of people are more intimately aware of what is expected in specific program areas. The process has served to create greater credibility and appreciation for what the Division of Student Affairs does. It has also been an educational tool for staff, providing renewal to those who have been in their positions for a long period of time and the opportunity for staff to become acquainted with the work of other individuals across the division. Staff feel that there is a greater positive change in program development, staff outlook, and availability of resources to meet needs of specific functional areas. CAS has been a valued assessment, evaluation, and planning tool for the Division of Student Affairs.

The outcomes of the process of self-assessment, evaluation, and planning, as described above, realistically depict the experiences of a single institution. The process utilized was stimulating, renewing, and challenging. Yet, to date, few institutions have initiated comprehensive processes of their own to operationalize the CAS standards and guidelines. As divisions of student affairs continue to seek collegial status within colleges and universities, CAS has provided an appropriate vehicle to pursue this effort. The purpose of this chapter is to motivate and help student affairs staff to take the standards off the bookshelf and put them into operation for program self-assessment, evaluation, and planning.

Some of the reasons for operationalizing the standards are to assist institutions in program development, accreditation self-study, staff development, program evaluation, enhancement of program credibility, education of the campus community, improvement in political maneuverability, and expansion of budget and staff.

Two approaches to operationalization have been described, compared, and contrasted. One approach is to utilize the CAS self-assessment guides, which are self-explanatory and comprehensive. Another approach is for selected task groups to address all components of each functional area by developing statements of what currently exists and recommendations for change or enhancement. Whichever process or combination is utilized, annual review is important in order to maintain the viability of the standards within each functional area.

One way to maintain the viability, as well as visibility, of the CAS standards and guidelines is to integrate them into department/division planning materials and annual reports. The reasons for this integration are to indicate compliance, to assist in moving beyond minimal compliance, and to provide impetus/motivation for change. In this chapter, the importance of planning was illustrated and an overview of common planning models was presented. The integration of CAS standards and guidelines into the planning model of UNCW was shown to be extremely smooth and successful. This approach utilizes CAS materials to develop annual departmental goals (key program results), problem-solving objectives, and innovative goals. This approach is also useful and appropriate for long-term planning.

The process of annual review of CAS materials is critical if the standards and guidelines are to function properly as working documents, as designed. For an institution not to operationalize the CAS standards and guidelines is to do a great disservice to the campus in general and to the student affairs division.

References

Aulepp, L., and Delworth, N. *Training Manual for an Ecosystem Model.* Boulder, Colo.: Western Interstate Commission for Higher Education, 1976.

Cope, R. G. *Opportunity from Strength: Strategic Planning Clarified with Case Examples.* ASHE-ERIC Higher Education Report No. 8. Washington, D.C.: Association for the Study of Higher Education, 1987.

Council for the Advancement of Standards for Student Services/Development Programs (CAS). *CAS Standards and Guidelines for Student Services/Development Programs.* Washington, D.C.: CAS, 1986.

Council for the Advancement of Standards for Student Services/Development Programs. *CAS Standards and Guidelines for Student Services/Development Programs: Student Orientation Programs Self Assessment Guide.* Washington, D.C.: CAS, 1988.

Deegan, A. X., and Fritz, R. J. *MBO Goes to College.* Boulder: University of Colorado, Division of Continuing Education, Bureau of Independent Study, 1975.

Drum, D. J., and Figler, H. E. *Outreach in Counseling.* New York: Intext Educational, 1973.

Erwin, T. D. "New Opportunities: How Student Affairs Can Contribute to Outcomes Assessment." In U. Delworth, G. R. Hanson, and Associates (eds.), *Student Services: A Handbook for the Profession.* (2nd ed.) San Francisco: Jossey-Bass, 1989.

Foxley, C. H. (ed.). *Applying Management Techniques.* New Directions for Student Services, no. 9. San Francisco: Jossey-Bass, 1980.

Harpel, R. L. "Planning, Budgeting, and Evaluation in Student Affairs Programs: A Manual for Administrators." In J. Eddy, J. Dameron, and D. T. Borland (eds.), *College Personnel Development, Administration, and Counseling.* (2nd ed.) Lanham, Md.: University Press of America, 1980.

Kaiser, L. R. "Campus Ecology: Implications for Environmental Design." Unpublished paper, Western Interstate Commission for Higher Education Task Force on Epidemiology, Campus Ecology, and Program Evaluation, Boulder, Colorado, 1972.

Lewis, M. D., and Lewis, J. A. "A Schematic for Change." *Personnel and Guidance Journal,* 1974, *52,* 320–323.

Miller, T. K., and Prince, J. S. *The Future of Student Affairs: A Guide to Student Development for Tomorrow's Higher Education.* San Francisco: Jossey-Bass, 1976.

Moore, M., and Delworth, U. *Training Manual for Student Service Program Development.* Boulder, Colo.: Western Interstate Commission for Higher Education, 1976.

Morrill, W. H., Oetting, E. R., and Hurst, J. C. "Dimensions of Counselor Functioning." *Personnel and Guidance Journal,* 1974, *52,* 354–359.

Scott, R. A. *Lords, Squires, and Yeomen: Collegiate Middle Managers and Their Organizations.* AAHE-ERIC Higher Education Report No. 7. Washington, D.C.: American Association for Higher Education, 1978.

Styles, M. H. "Effective Models of Systematic Program Planning." In M. J. Barr, L. A.

Keating, and Associates, *Developing Effective Student Services Programs.* San Francisco: Jossey-Bass, 1985.

Tincher, W. A. "Time Management and Planning for Student Affairs Professionals." In T. K. Miller, R. B. Winston, and W. R. Mendenhall (eds.), *Administration and Leadership in Student Affairs: Actualizing Student Development in Higher Education.* Muncie, Ind.: Accelerated Development, 1983.

William A. Bryan is vice-chancellor for student affairs and professor of educational design and management at the University of North Carolina, Wilmington. He has served as president of the American College Personnel Association.

Richard H. Mullendore is associate vice-chancellor for student affairs at the University of North Carolina, Wilmington, and president of the National Orientation Directors Association. He has presented papers at state, regional, and national conferences on operationalizing CAS standards and guidelines in the campus setting.

Professional standards and guidelines are of special value in the area of academic preparation, for it is in this arena that the seeds of professional practice are initially planted. It is essential that those who aspire to become professional student affairs practitioners and educators receive the best preparation possible. Preparation standards are the essential foundation for quality education, and it is important that professionals know and understand how to apply standards to the educational process.

Using Standards in Professional Preparation

Theodore K. Miller

At least three types of professional standards have great utility as educational tools and developmental guides for the preparation of aspiring professional practitioners in the field of student affairs. Two of these, ethical standards and standards of professional practice, reflect the desired behaviors and appropriate activities of professional practitioners in their daily work, while the third represents standards of professional preparation. This chapter's primary focus is on the latter, though I touch on the educational potential of the former two as well. The three preparation tracks—counseling, administrative, and developmental—are described and critiqued, and the accreditation process for academic programs through the Council for the Accreditation of Counseling and Related Educational Programs (CACREP) is discussed.

Historical Perspective

Historically, standards for the professional education of student affairs practitioners are of relatively recent vintage, largely being developed during the past two decades. Surely, there were, earlier, several well-conceived guides designed to establish the philosophical foundations of formal student affairs practice and, implicitly therefore, preparation. Indeed, the concern for establishing a comprehensive student affairs philosophy is still with us (National Association of Student Personnel Administrators [NASPA], 1987; Whitt, Carnaghi, Matkin, Scalese-Love, and Nestor, 1990). In 1937 and again in 1949 the American Council on Education (ACE) sponsored committees of concerned professionals to examine the nature of the field, which resulted in two publications (ACE, 1937, 1949). Although not designed or intended as standards per se, these statements represent early attempts to identify and postulate basic principles to guide student affairs practice.

A move closer to the establishment of standards of professional preparation was the work of the Council of Student Personnel Associations in Higher Education (COSPA), founded in December 1963 as an outgrowth of the Inter-Association Coordinating Committee, which had nine member associations and one affiliate member (Hardee, n.d.). In February 1964 the COSPA Joint Commission on Professional Development submitted to the profession at large for its consideration the document "A Proposal for Professional Preparation in College Student Personnel Work," which went through numerous revisions during subsequent years. As an example, "Guidelines for Graduate Programs in the Preparation of Student Personnel Workers in Higher Education" was drafted by COSPA (1967) in collaboration with the Interdivisional Committee of the American Personnel and Guidance Association. The change in title from "proposal for" in the 1964 version to "guidelines for" in the 1967 fourth-draft revision exemplifies the movement from a rather tentative statement of what professional preparation should entail to one asserting specific guidelines that should be followed in graduate education programs. A final statement, popularly recognized as the "COSPA Report," was actually published some time after the dissolution of the council (COSPA, 1975).

During this same time period, others concerned with the graduate education of counselors and other professional helpers were busy developing counselor education standards and exploring the possibilities for accrediting graduate academic programs. One of the prime moving forces in this domain was the Association for Counselor Education and Supervision (ACES), a division of the American Personnel and Guidance Association (APGA) later to be renamed the American Association for Counseling and Development. By 1973 ACES had sponsored the creation of a set of professional standards that could be used to accredit counseling and personnel services education programs (ACES, 1973). APGA had recognized ACES as its official counselor education accrediting body and moved to establish an interassociation committee to guide counselor education program accreditation activity and the review and revision of the ACES/APGA preparation standards.

In response to the ACES/APGA initiative to create both standards and an accreditation vehicle for counselors and other personnel services specialists, the American College Personnel Association (ACPA) established an ad hoc Preparation Standards Statement Drafting Committee to develop a proposed set of standards that would adequately and appropriately incorporate the special concerns of student affairs graduate education within the ACES/APGA format. In its March 1979 meeting (ACPA, 1980), the ACPA Executive Council adopted the committee's statement, "Standards for the Preparation of Counselors and College Student Affairs Specialists at the

Master's Degree Level," as the official ACPA preparation standards. ACPA then initiated a two-pronged thrust in the area of professional standards. One was a collaborative effort with NASPA to establish a profession-wide program of standards development, and the other was a concerted effort to work under the APGA organizational umbrella to establish an agency for the accreditation of counselor education and student affairs education preparation programs. The former initiative resulted in the creation of the Council for the Advancement of Standards for Student Services/Development Programs (CAS), and the latter in the establishment of CACREP, an academic program accrediting agency now recognized by the Council on Postsecondary Accreditation (COPA) as the official accrediting agency for counselor and student affairs education programs.

Both the CAS (1986b) and CACREP (1988) preparation standards reflect the influence of the ACPA standards for student affairs preparation. This influence is particularly obvious when one recognizes that both have incorporated the three academic emphases common to student affairs preparation programs—counseling, administrative, and developmental (Rodgers, 1977)—which were prominently incorporated into the 1979 ACPA document.

Although ACPA worked closely with CACREP from its inception, it was not until the 1985 revision of the CACREP preparation standards that the student affairs focus was incorporated therein. This fact reflects the differences of opinion that existed between counselor educators and student affairs educators in the early 1980s. That difference might be best defined by the issues inherent to the question of whether counselor education implicitly incorporates all the essentials of student affairs education within its core curriculum or whether student affairs practice calls for a unique curriculum that differs in some ways at least from that of counselor education. From the beginning, the contention of most student affairs educators has been that counseling, important as it is to the helping professions, is not sufficient unto itself to be the only curriculum of choice for the preparation of professional student affairs practitioners. Both the 1985 revisions and the 1988 version of the CACREP standards suggest that this position is becoming an accepted norm for those involved in professional preparation. It is hoped that the 1993 revision of the CACREP standards, which is currently underway, will reinforce this position to an even greater extent so that the profession may achieve parity in counselor education and student affairs education program accreditation.

Making Meaning of Professional Preparation Standards

Standards and guidelines for professional preparation tend to follow established patterns common to standards of professional practice in that they may include both requirements and recommendations. Requirements, which represent behavior or conditions *essential* to compliance with the standards, use the auxiliary verbs *must* and *shall*. Recommendations or guidelines, on the other hand, are intended to clarify and amplify the standards and are not viewed as essential to compliance with the standards. Although they may be integrated with requirements in the text, recommendations use the auxiliary verbs *should* and *may*. It is important, when attempting to implement the standards, that the distinction between standards (requirements) and guidelines (recommendations) be clearly understood. There are arguments that guidelines alone are adequate to steer professional preparation and practice.

A major value of preparation standards to the profession is that they provide criteria by which academic programs of professional preparation can be judged. Whether used for accreditation or program development purposes, standards allow faculty, staff, administrators, and students alike to measure a particular program's characteristics against a set of well-conceived criteria that, subject to compliance, represent at least a minimal level of quality assurance and educational effectiveness. Standards, in fact, have great utility for enhancing educational quality in that they provide an avenue for continuous self-study and review, a primary purpose of accreditation (Council on Postsecondary Accreditation [COPA], 1989).

Who has responsibility for formulating and disseminating standards for the preparation of student affairs professionals? Largely, the answer is the profession as a whole or those agencies that best represent the interests of the profession at large. Standards may be developed by individual professional associations such as ACPA and NASPA, or by umbrella associations such as the American Association for Counseling and Development and the American Psychological Association, or more desirably, by councils or other agencies such as COSPA, CACREP, and the Council for the Advancement of Standards for Student Services/Development Programs (CAS) that, as interassociation consortiums, reflect collaborative efforts by a broad segment of the profession at large. The broader and more comprehensive the foundations underlying a set of professional standards, the more credibility and utility they have. A set of standards that reflects the thinking of the profession at large, as opposed to that of one organization within the profession, will have much more credibility among potential users in that such standards reflect a degree of consensual validity that cannot otherwise exist. The entity that proposes and disseminates the standards does make a difference as to whether or not they will be recognized and used.

Why should student affairs faculty be concerned about using preparation standards in their academic programs? Although an academic program obviously reflects the quality of its faculty, curriculum, learning environment, students, and support systems, that correspondence alone is not necessarily sufficient to motivate all the people involved to seek improvements in the quality of their collective educational enterprise. There is, however, at least one motivating factor that can provide reasons beyond individual preference for increasing the quality of educational programs. That factor is social recognition, both general and peer. It is the rare faculty member who desires to be intimately associated with a poor-quality academic program that few students find educationally challenging, that even fewer professional colleagues recognize as academically reputable, that institutional administrators are not willing to support, and that the larger campus community disdains. Probably the single best way to obtain assurance that an academic program is substantially accomplishing its educational objectives is to document with reasonable evidence that the program merits recognition for academic worth and social value.

The Accreditation Option

Professional standards are the best available criteria to use in making objective judgments about program quality, and accreditation is in all likelihood the most credible vehicle currently devised to evidence that educational quality prevails (Young, Chambers, Kells, and Associates, 1983). As noted by the Council on Postsecondary Accreditation (COPA, 1989, p. 3), "accreditation is a system for recognizing educational institutions and professional programs affiliated with those institutions for a level of performance, integrity, and quality which entitles them to the confidence of the educational community and the public they serve." Further, accreditation is viewed by COPA (1989, p. 35) as existing for the primary purpose of validating programs "which are generally accepted as preparing for the entry level(s) into a profession" to assure the public that program graduates possess the basic knowledge and skills prerequisite to practice successfully in that professional arena. Consequently, a general rule is that programs at the baccalaureate or master's level will undergo accreditation whereas advanced degree programs in the same area will not, except in instances where initial entrance into the profession calls for a doctorate. CACREP's accreditation of counselor education and supervision doctoral programs is based on the rationale that the doctoral level is the entrance level for counselor educators and supervisors, similar to the rationale used by the Committee on Accreditation of the American Psychological Association for accrediting counseling psychology programs, among others.

In effect, entry-level academic programs that can reasonably document substantial compliance with professional standards that have been agreed upon by the profession at large receive general and peer recognition not awarded to those who cannot evidence that compliance. Achievement of accreditation status, therefore, might well be one of the best ways to use professional standards in a student affairs preparation program.

How is accreditation obtained for an academic program? Very carefully might be a reasonable answer, but currently the options are indeed limited for student affairs preparation programs. COPA (1989) identifies fifty-five accrediting bodies as members of its umbrella postsecondary accreditation organization. These include nine regional and six national agencies that accredit at the institutional level only and forty specialized accrediting agencies that accredit academic programs rather than institutions. Of the forty speciality areas, only one is currently authorized to accredit student affairs in higher education preparation programs. That accrediting body is CACREP (address: 5999 Stevenson Avenue, Alexandria, Virginia 22304; telephone: 703-823-9800, ext. 301). CACREP is authorized to accredit master's degree programs designed to prepare individuals for community counseling, mental health counseling, school counseling, student affairs practice in higher education, and doctoral-level programs in counselor education and supervision (COPA, 1989).

The fact that CACREP is presently the only COPA-recognized agency accrediting student affairs preparation programs is somewhat problematic, especially for faculty members in programs that are not philosophically derived from a counseling orientation or are not organizationally associated with a counselor education department. Consequently, faculty members from such programs often feel discomfort with CACREP because they view it as a counselor-oriented accrediting agency that neither understands nor appreciates the unique nature of student affairs preparation as distinct from counselor education. An inverse relationship appears to exist in that the greater the curricular emphasis on student affairs administration or student development within a particular program, the less likely its faculty members are to view CACREP as a viable accreditation option. This is unfortunate for several reasons, not the least of which is CACREP's responsiveness to the special views and needs of those responsible for the education of student affairs practitioners. It is likely, however, that preparation program faculties who hold student affairs administration as their primary academic emphasis will require considerable persuasion that CACREP is in fact an appropriate vehicle for accreditation purposes. This viewpoint, in all likelihood, was at the core of the recent proposal by the ACPA-NASPA Task Force on Professional Preparation and Practice (1989, p. 37) to establish a national-level "study group to make recommendations on the accreditation of preparation programs and credentialing or establishing a registry of professionals in student affairs." Such a study group could have a major impact on the CACREP standards and accreditation processes, especially now as that accrediting agency is reviewing and open to amending its standards, policies, and procedures.

The idea of establishing a registry, although not directly connected with accrediting preparation programs, has utility for recognizing and certifying qualified practitioners to obtain employment in the field. Employers of prospective program graduates could use both accreditation and certification as hiring criteria in that the former would ensure that employees have received a quality professional education and the latter, through a formal registry assessment vehicle, that they are qualified by knowledge and skill to be gainfully employed in a professional student affairs work setting.

Accrediting Student Affairs Programs

Even though it took several years of ardent discussion within CACREP to arrive at a decision to integrate the Environmental and Specialty Standards for Student Affairs Practice in Higher Education (CACREP, 1988) into its standards, the task has been accomplished and specialty area standards are in place. These standards provide for not only a counseling curricular emphasis for student affairs preparation programs but developmental and administrative emphases as well. Consequently, it is now quite feasible for graduate programs with a focus on student development or student affairs administration to be accredited through CACREP. These options open many doors previously locked to student affairs preparation programs in the area of accreditation recognition. It is, in effect, no longer possible to argue that there is no COPA-recognized agency to review and accredit student affairs preparation programs that are not primarily counselor-oriented in nature. This fact does not mean, however, that all program accreditation issues in student affairs are resolved at this point. Quite the contrary, there is much work to be done, especially in the area of standards review and development.

Curriculum Standards. Currently, the CACREP standards, as revised in 1988, recognize the special and unique needs and concerns of student affairs preparation in the areas of curricular and clinical instruction. The former is handled by providing three different curricular emphases for student affairs programs. These include the counseling emphasis, the developmental emphasis, and the administrative emphasis, which are based on the ACPA and CAS preparation standards that used Rodgers's (1977) research findings as a model. Each of these three program emphases has an unique curricular core that focuses on the special knowledge and skills identified as most relevant and essential to the particular area of specialization involved. The student affairs counseling emphasis incorporates basically the same criteria that make up the eight common-core curricular areas for school and community counseling programs, yet adds three additional components. The developmental and administrative emphases incorporate some of these same areas but place them in different configurations with other, more relevant curricular areas. These CACREP curricular emphases, which largely reflect the current CAS preparation standards as well, are reported in Table 1.

The formal curriculum content of each of the three program emphases was designed to focus attention on both the general and special knowledge and skills most relevant to it. Consequently, there is overlap among the three curricula because of the student clientele and educational environ-

Table 1. CACREP Student Affairs Preparation Standards: Required Core Curriculum by Program Emphasis

Counseling	*Administrative*	*Developmental*
1. Human growth and development	1. Higher education and development personnel functions	1. Higher education and student development functions
2. Social and cultural foundations	2. Human development theory and practice	2. The American college student and the college environment
3. Helping relationships	3. Organizational behavior and development	3. Organizational behavior and development
4. Groups	4. Administration	4. Research and evaluation
5. Lifestyle and career development	5. Research and evaluation	5. Human development theory and practice
6. Appraisal	6. Administrative uses of computers	6. Helping relationships and career development
7. Research and evaluation		
8. Professional orientation		
9. Higher education		
10. Student affairs functions		
11. Student development applications		

Source: Council for the Accreditation of Counseling and Related Educational Programs (CACREP), 1988.

ments held in common. Nevertheless, because the recipients of the education provided by these programs are employed to carry out different functions upon graduation, the knowledge content to which they are exposed must be in some ways different. It was precisely these identified similarities and differences that resulted in a tripartite curricular approach that holds human development theory, research and evaluation, higher education, and student affairs/student development functions in common but provides exposure to special knowledge and skills required for successful practice in the particular types of positions that graduates from a given program will hold. One might argue that in order to achieve a fully comprehensive professional education, students should become learned in all three of the curricular content areas. Such an extensive education, however, would be largely unrealistic because of the extreme costs and time commitments required for students, programs and faculties alike. Student affairs programs of high quality require the employment of staff members who possess the professional knowledge and skills essential to carrying out the many and diverse responsibilities involved, but the reality is, at the entry level at least, that individual staff members cannot be expected to know and apply the skills all equally well. Therefore, diversity in professional education must be recognized as essential to providing the profession as a whole with well-qualified individuals who can carry out the multiplicity of responsibilities called for by such a comprehensive enterprise.

Supervised Practice. Student affairs preparation programs can be construed as reflecting a practice-oriented, as opposed to a research-oriented, focus because their primary purpose is to provide students with the knowledge and skills required for positions in professional student affairs and related educational support services in institutions of higher learning. Consequently, a major thrust of this professional education includes supervised fieldwork. As described in Table 2, the CACREP standards specify that a required minimum of tutorial instruction be provided through both practicum and internship experiences. These clinical experiences may be obtained in a wide variety of counseling, student development, and student affairs administration assignments, each of which is largely determined by a given program's curricular emphasis, available placements with qualified on-site supervision, and the career interests that the students wish to pursue. Support for the establishment of such placement sites is provided by ACPA Ethical Standard 1.25, which states that as ACPA members, student affairs professionals will "support professional preparation program efforts by providing assistantships, practica, field placements, and consultation to students and faculty (ACPA, 1990, p. 14).

Many of these fieldwork placements may be located directly at the preparation program's parent institution, with on-site supervision being provided by campus student affairs officers. Limiting fieldwork assignments to one institution, however, is not especially desirable because this may tend to promote an orthodoxy of viewpoint, philosophy, and organizational bias when all students are exposed to similar experiences. Granted, the larger and more decentralized the campus, the less likely an orthodoxy will develop, but a good principle to follow is that the more diverse the opportunities for practical learning, the better the preparation program. An excellent internship program and model has been developed by the Association of College and University Housing Officers-International ([ACUHO-I] 1986). The ACUHO-I housing internships provide students with opportunities to spend one academic term, a minimum of eight weeks, working in a selected college or university's housing office. Students are assigned to these internships on a competitive basis under the auspices of the ACUHO-I Housing Internship Committee and receive a moderate travel allowance and a monthly stipend of no less than minimum wage. Although these internships are limited to housing operations, the ACPA-NASPA Task Force on Professional Preparation and Practice (1989) has recommended that a national clearinghouse for summer fieldwork experiences for student affairs graduate students be established. Such a program would expose students to student affairs practice at institutions different from those in which they are taking their degrees, yet provide them with the opportunity to obtain internship degree credit on their home campuses. Even if such programs are not immediately available, a preparation program of quality should enable a student to obtain an off-campus internship if it will enhance his or her education.

Table 2. CACREP Student Affairs Preparation Standards: Required Clinical Experience by Program Emphasis

Counseling	*Administrative*	*Developmental*
Supervised Counseling Practicum	*Supervised Administrative Practicum*[a]	*Supervised Developmental Practicum*[a]
Individual and group counseling focus Requires minimum of 100 total clock hours 40 hours of direct client contact 1 hour per week individual supervision 1.5 hours per week group supervision	Focus on student affairs management and programming, including organization development Requires minimum of 100 total clock hours 15 hours direct service work with clientele appropriate to the program area 1 hour per week individual supervision 1.5 hours per week group supervision	Focus on student development interventions, including organization development Includes counseling pre-practicum laboratories Requires minimum of 100 total clock hours 15 hours direct service work with clientele appropriate to the program area 1 hour per week individual supervision 1.5 hours per week group supervision
Supervised Counseling Internship	*Supervised Administrative Internship*[a]	*Supervised Student Development Internship*[a]
Subsequent to practicum experience Individual and group counseling focus Requires minimum of 600 total clock hours 240 hours of direct client contact 1 hour per week individual supervision 1.5 hours per week group supervision	Focus on student affairs management and programming Requires minimum of 600 total clock hours[b] 60 hours direct service work with clientele appropriate to the program area 1 hour per week individual supervision 1.5 hours per week group supervision	Focus on student affairs developmental programming, including organizational development Requires minimum of 600 total clock hours[b] 60 hours direct service work with clientele appropriate to the program area 1 hour per week individual supervision 1.5 hours per week group supervision

[a]Students' supervised fieldwork includes experience in at least two different student affairs placements during the course of their practica/internship experience.

[b]Up to 300 clock hours (50 percent) of the student affairs internship requirement may be earned through professionally supervised graduate assistantship assignments in appropriate work settings.

Source: Council for the Accreditation of Counseling and Related Educational Programs (CACREP), 1988.

As Table 2 denotes, there are three primary requirements that students in supervised practice placements must meet. First, they must spend a particular number of clock hours working in the assigned area, a specified number of which include direct contact with the clientele served by the office or program. Second, students must receive both individual and group supervision by well-qualified on-site authorities or faculty members. Third, the field placement must be in a laboratory, office, program, or related work setting that provides an opportunity to practice and learn the work responsibilities and skills typically performed by regularly employed staff members in that particular professional work setting. A special CACREP standards option allows students who receive equivalent supervised practical work experiences through graduate assistantships or similar work assignments in student affairs programs to thereby satisfy the internship requirement (CACREP, 1988).

Special consideration in the standards is given to the quality of supervision required. As previously noted, the standards call for well-qualified on-site staff members or program faculty to provide clinical supervision on both individual and group bases. Well qualified, in this instance, is defined on the basis of certain specified criteria that are relevant for student affairs settings but that tend to be framed in terminology more common to counselor education than to student affairs education. These supervisory eligibility criteria include (1) for program faculty members, those who hold doctoral degrees in counselor education or closely related professional specialities or who are receiving supervision from one with such a degree, have had relevant professional experience, and possess demonstrated competence in counseling or human development at levels appropriate for the students supervised in the placement setting; (2) for graduate students, those who have completed a minimum of two practica and one internship in equivalent assignments and who are themselves supervised by program faculty; and (3) for on-site supervisors, those who have earned, at minimum, a master's degree in the program emphasis area, who possess appropriate certifications or licenses, who have at least two years of pertinent professional experience, and who are well apprised of the program's expectations, requirements, and evaluation procedures for students in fieldwork positions (CACREP, 1988). Unfortunately, these criteria tend to be worded in terms more appropriate for counseling than for student affairs administration, thereby promoting discomfort among the faculty of student affairs programs. It is standards like these, which must be translated for use in a parallel arena, that encourage student affairs administrators and educators to recommend that more definitive standards for student affairs fieldwork experience be established (ACPA-NASPA Task Force on Professional Preparation and Practice, 1989).

Functional Area Standards of Practice

Until recently there have been few comprehensive, well-established, and agreed-upon standards of practice to guide the work of student affairs practitioners. In 1986 CAS adopted sixteen functional area standards and guidelines for professional practice, with three additional sets of functional area standards adopted subsequently (CAS, 1986a, 1987; Miller, Neuberger, McEwen, White, and Thomas, 1990) (see Table 3). As described elsewhere (Mable, this volume), these standards have since been incorporated into *CAS Self Assessment Guides* (Miller, Thomas, Looney, and Yerian, 1988), which can be used for self-study purposes. These guides present a set of criterion measures that can be used to judge how well a program is in compliance with the standards and to provide a systematic process by which professional staff members can evaluate the quality and effectiveness of their programs through self-study initiatives. The standards and self-assessment guides, which are operational versions of the functional area standards, inform both students and staff members alike about the characteristics that are desirable and essential to high-quality student affairs practice.

For both preparation and staff development purposes, the CAS self-assessment guides can be used in at least three ways as educational tools. First, they make an excellent vehicle to provide information that describes in some detail a quality program of practice. Reading, reviewing, and discussing with colleagues the individual guides and the functional area standards included in the appendix of each increases the awareness and understanding of the component parts essential to the given student affairs program under study. These guides can provide an excellent introduction to a functional program area with which a student or staff member is unfamiliar.

Second, the guides are an excellent vehicle for providing students in practica or internships a framework to review and learn about the program areas to which they are assigned. The standards help students to frame appropriate questions for discussions with their supervisors, and they also can

Table 3. CAS Functional Area Standards and Guidelines

Academic Advising	Housing and Residential Life
Admission Programs and Services	Judicial Programs and Services
Career Planning and Placement	Learning Assistance Programs
College Unions	Minority Student Programs and Services
Commuter Student Programs and Services	Recreational Sports
Counseling Services	Religious Programs
Disabled Student Services	Research and Evaluation
Division Level Programs	Student Activities
Fraternity and Sorority Advising	Student Orientation
	Women Student Programs and Services

Sources: Council for the Advancement of Standards for Student Services/Development Programs, (CAS) 1986a, 1987; Miller, Neuberger, McEwen, White, and Thomas, 1990.

be used by supervisors to structure the fieldwork experience to better ensure that the students receive a comprehensive overview of the program as well as learn specific skills.

Third, the guides assign students or staff members the responsibility of applying the standards. Some preparation programs, for instance, require students to complete mini-self-studies of their practica and internship placements as a way to better comprehend the functional area to which they are assigned, as well as to learn to apply the standards in practical ways. The more students learn about how to use professional standards and guidelines in their graduate programs, the greater their ability to understand and use them upon graduation. In some instances these same individuals will be asked to inform and instruct staff member colleagues in the use of professional standards in their employment situations after graduation because they will be more familiar with and knowledgeable about applying the standards in practical work settings. Strong arguments can be made for the utility of exposing students to the existence and use of ethical standards such as the Statement of Ethical Principles and Standards (ACPA, 1990) as well. It should go without saying that a high-quality program of professional education in student affairs will expose its students to the many facets of professional standards and guidelines. CAS has published a training manual (Yerian and Miller, 1989) designed to instruct students and practitioners in the use of *CAS Standards and Guidelines* (CAS, 1986a) and *CAS Assessment Guides* (Miller, Thomas, Looney, and Yerian, 1988). This manual provides both a script and transparency masters that can be used for instruction purposes.

Issues and Alternatives

Preparation program standards, similar to any professional norms or guidelines, must be reviewed periodically and revised from time to time in response to the changes occurring in the profession. It is important to recognize that student affairs practice is extremely complex, is rapidly changing, is expected to provide multiple and varied applications, is influenced by a number of newly conceptualized developmental and management theories, and requires that its practitioners work for institutions of higher learning rather than be self-employed. Because of these complicating factors, the practice presents the profession at large and its preparation programs with a dilemma: There is no single best education to prepare all entry-level practitioners for the field. Some positions call for high levels of interpersonal advising skills, while others call for competent administrative leadership and management. There is a need for institutional research and program evaluation, on the one hand, and environmental intervention strategy planning and implementation, on the other. Some programs call for special knowledge and skills in small group practice, while others require high levels of individual counseling competence. Some situations demand the capacity to instruct and coach students and staff, while others specify the ability to personally operationalize theory into practice.

Budget analysis and planning, resource management, written reports, oral presentations, enrollment management, organizational development, strategic planning, data base development and management, comprehension of paradigmatic shifts, and a multitude of diverse functional responsibilities are all part and parcel of the professional baggage of student affairs practitioners. In effect, there are many more areas of expertise demanded than any one individual could possibly master, even with a lifetime of continuous education. Entry-level practitioners who hope to survive and prosper in this complex milieu, therefore, *must possess both general knowledge of the many dimensions involved and expertise in one or more of these dimensions.* Because of this broad-based demand, no single academic preparation program can be expected to adequately educate prospective practitioners in all of these areas at once. It therefore behooves the designers of preparation programs to identify the minimal level of general knowledge and skill required of all professionals and the particular areas of expertise they can best help students master during the relatively short duration of entry-level programs of study. In all likelihood, any program that seeks to be all things to all entry-level students will fail rather spectacularly in such an educational endeavor.

It is for precisely this reason that the preparation standards devised by ACPA, CAS, and CACREP incorporated the tripartite emphasis approach referred to previously. The inherent complexity of the profession reinforces the importance of having different programs provide alternative emphases and opportunities for students who seek to establish careers in the field of student affairs. Likewise, it is essential that periodic reviews of the preparation standards be initiated to ensure incorporation of the new and diverse aspects of knowledge and practice required for entrance into a field that is constantly adapting to changes in the larger society. An example of these changes is reflected in the recommendation by Johnson and Sandeen (1988) that because the majority of student affairs preparation programs originated in counselor education departments and have consequently tended to delimit administrative theory in their curricula, there should be a systematic de-emphasis on counselor-oriented student affairs preparation programs. These authors reiterated the position of Forney and Gilroy (1986), who questioned the responsiveness of preparation programs to the fine-tuning needed to accommodate societal and institutional changes. Johnson and Sandeen (1988, p. 82) make a significant point when they note that both preparation programs and the guidelines and standards that support them need to view program curricula "through the filter of the future" to better ensure that entry-level professionals will be prepared to meet the challenge of change. It is essential that program faculty and professional leaders alike seek to find ways to better assure the profession, society at large, and the students who seek careers in student affairs that the education received is high quality and relevant.

Another issue that the field of student affairs needs to face squarely is its intra-institutional relationships to academic affairs and educational support service programs. A decade and a half ago Miller and Prince (1976) proposed an organizational configuration designed to integrate student affairs with academic affairs so that the student clientele would be exposed to holistic educational experiences. The very fact that *CAS Standards and Guidelines* (CAS, 1986a) includes academic advising, learning assistance programs, and research and evaluation among its functional areas suggests implicit connections between the two typically separate administrative areas. How well, if at all, preparation programs provide opportunities for students to connect the two arenas in theory and in practice is of paramount concern for the future of the field. Increasingly, there are staff programs within academic units in which practitioners directly provide student support services such as admissions, counseling, advising, activities, and job placement to the students matriculating in a particular academic unit. Just as there is a strong need for student affairs practitioners and preparation program faculty to interact in their joint efforts (ACPA-NASPA Task Force on Professional Preparation and Practice, 1989), there is an equally important need for student affairs preparation to provide students with connections to the campus academic arena as well.

The issue of fieldwork practice, placement, and supervision is an ever-present concern for it is usually through fieldwork experiences that students develop their most lasting impressions of the role and function of student affairs practice on college campuses. There is little doubt that preparation standards call for a diligent effort from faculty and staff in this area of endeavor, but it is also clear that the professional standards must focus to an even greater extent on the quality, as opposed to the quantity, of supervised experience. As noted earlier, the ACPA-NASPA Task Force on Professional Preparation and Practice (1989) called for increased efforts to establish standards with appropriate criterion measures to guide the selection and retention of well-qualified fieldwork supervisors. Too often the quality of the practical learning that students receive from their practica and internships is left to the judgment of practitioners who are ill-prepared and highly limited in time when they serve as students' tutors, coaches, and supervisors. The qualifications of those who supervise fieldwork are no less important than those of the faculty who teach the academic material.

Finally, quality assurance is perhaps the most significant issue now facing the professional preparation of student affairs practitioners. Both personal and intellectual characteristics and capacities are essential to the selection and retention of student affairs personnel (Miller, 1988), and the professional standards do not presently provide, and may never be able to provide, a clear delineation of what those essential professional qualities are or should be. Standards can, however, provide impetus for establishing at least minimal criteria of quality and encouraging responsible parties to follow through on making the important judgments required for both the selection and the deselection process. Professional standards establish the norms for a profession. Members of the profession have an ethical obligation to follow those standards as rigorously as possible or to systematically amend the standards to better assure the profession, the public, and the students that the end result of the educational process reflects high-quality practice to the betterment of all concerned. Resisting or rejecting the standards that the profession has established to guide practice and preparation is not a professional activity of merit. The professional standards currently in place to guide the education of student affairs practitioners are admittedly imperfect in their present forms, but they are the best vehicle for assuring students, institutions of higher learning, and society at large that the field of student affairs is a profession of character and high-quality practice.

References

American College Personnel Association (ACPA). "A Summary of the Minutes of the Executive Council Meeting, March 29, 1979." *Journal of College Student Personnel,* 1980, *21,* 182–184.

American College Personnel Association. "Statement of Ethical Principles and Standards." *Journal of College Student Development,* 1990, *31,* 11–16.

American College Personnel Association-National Association of Student Personnel Administrators (NASPA) Task Force on Professional Preparation and Practice. *The Recruitment, Preparation, and Nurturing of the Student Affairs Professional.* Washington, D.C.: ACPA-NASPA, 1989.

American Council on Education (ACE). *The Student Personnel Point of View.* American Council on Education Studies, series 1, vol. 1, no. 3. Washington, D.C.: ACE, 1937.

American Council on Education. *The Student Personnel Point of View.* American Council on Education Studies, series 6, vol. 13, no. 13. Washington, D.C.: ACE, 1949.

Association of College and University Housing Officers-International. *Handy Hints for Developing a Housing Internship Program.* (Brochure.) Gainesville, Fla.: Housing Internship Committee, 1986.

Association of Counselor Educators and Supervisors (ACES). *Standards for the Preparation of Counselors and Other Personnel Services Specialists at the Master's Degree Level.* Washington, D.C.: ACES, 1973.

Council for the Accreditation of Counseling and Related Educational Programs (CACREP). *Accreditation Procedures Manual and Application for Counseling and Related Educational Programs.* (Rev. ed.) Alexandria, Va.: CACREP, 1985.

Council for the Accreditation of Counseling and Related Educational Programs. *Accreditation Procedures Manual and Application.* Alexandria, Va.: CACREP, 1988.

Council for the Advancement of Standards for Student Services/Development Programs (CAS). *CAS Standards and Guidelines for Student Services/Development Programs.* Washington, D.C.: CAS, 1986a.

Council for the Advancement of Standards for Student Services/Development Programs. "Preparation Standards and Guidelines at the Master's Degree Level for Student Services/Development Professionals in Postsecondary Education." In

CAS Standards and Guidelines for Student Services/Development Programs. Washington, D.C.: CAS, 1986b.

Council for the Advancement of Standards for Student Services/Development Programs. *CAS Standards and Guidelines for Admission Programs and Services.* Washington, D.C.: CAS, 1987.

Council of Student Personnel Associations (COSPA). "A Proposal for Professional Preparation in College Student Personnel Work." Unpublished manuscript, Indianapolis, Indiana, February 1964.

Council of Student Personnel Associations. "Guidelines for Graduate Programs in the Preparation of Student Personnel Workers in Higher Education." Unpublished manuscript, Washington, D.C., March 5, 1967.

Council of Student Personnel Associations. "Student Development Services in Post-Secondary Education." *Journal of College Student Personnel,* 1975, *16* (6), 524–528.

Council on Postsecondary Accreditation (COPA). *The COPA Handbook.* Washington, D.C.: COPA, 1989.

Forney, R., and Gilroy, M. "Impressions and Issues Regarding Master's Preparation." *NASPA Region II Newsletter,* 1986, *6* (3), 4–5.

Hardee, M. D. *COSPA: The Council of Student Personnel Associations in Higher Education.* (Brochure.) Tallahassee, Fla.: COSPA, n.d.

Johnson, C. S., and Sandeen, A. "Relationship of Guidelines and Standards of Student Affairs Preparation Programs to Current and Future Trends." In R. B. Young and L. V. Moore (eds.), *The State of the Art of Professional Education and Practice.* Washington, D.C.: American College Personnel Association, National Association of Student Personnel Administrators, and the Association for Counselor Education and Supervision, 1988.

Miller, T. K. "Challenge, Support, and Response: An Epilogue." In R. B. Young and L. V. Moore (eds.), *The State of the Art of Professional Education and Practice.* Washington, D.C.: American College Personnel Association, National Association of Student Personnel Administrators, and the Association of Counselor Education and Supervision, 1988.

Miller, T. K., Neuberger, C. G., McEwen, M., White, E., and Thomas, W. L. *Women Student Programs and Services Self Assessment Guide.* Washington, D.C.: Council for the Advancement of Standards for Student Services/Development Programs, 1990.

Miller, T. K., and Prince, J. S. *The Future of Student Affairs: A Guide to Student Development for Tomorrow's Higher Education.* San Francisco: Jossey-Bass, 1976.

Miller, T. K., Thomas, W. L., Looney, S. C., and Yerian, J. *CAS Self Assessment Guides.* Washington, D.C.: Council for the Advancement of Standards for Student Services/Development Programs, 1988.

National Association of Student Personnel Administrators (NASPA). *A Perspective on Student Affairs: A Statement Issued on the 50th Anniversary of the Student Personnel Point of View.* Washington, D.C.: NASPA, 1987.

Rodgers, R. F. "Student Personnel Work as Social Intervention." In G. H. Knock (ed.), *Perspectives on the Preparation of Student Affairs Professionals.* Washington, D.C.: American College Personnel Association, 1977.

Whitt, E. J., Carnaghi, J. E., Matkin, J., Scalese-Love, P., and Nestor, D. "Believing Is Seeing: Alternative Perspectives on a Statement of Professional Philosophy for Student Affairs." *NASPA Journal,* 1990, *27* (3), 178–184.

Yerian, J. M., and Miller, T. K. *Putting the CAS Standards to Work: Training Manual for the CAS Self Assessment Guides.* Washington, D.C.: Council for the Advancement of Standards for Student Services/Development Programs, 1989.

Young, K. E., Chambers, C. M., Kells, H. R., and Associates. *Understanding Accreditation: Contemporary Perspectives on Issues and Practices in Evaluating Educational Quality.* San Francisco: Jossey-Bass, 1983.

Theodore K. Miller is professor and coordinator of the Student Personnel in Higher Education Program at the University of Georgia, Athens.

In order to apply professional practice standards systematically, it is first necessary to establish what is happening, decide what are the desired outcomes, and evaluate the effects that programs and services have on students and staff.

Standards and Outcomes Assessment: Strategies and Tools

Roger B. Winston, Jr., William S. Moore

A hallmark of the student affairs field during the past two decades has been a push toward increased professionalism, which has necessitated the formulation of a new mission that goes beyond the mere provision of support services for the academic development of college students and the maintenance of discipline. This redefinition of the student affairs mission, based on an understanding and application of principles of student development that were both complementary and of equal importance to academic learning, began first with the work of the Council of Student Personnel Associations ([COSPA] 1972) and the American College Personnel Association's THE (Tomorrow's Higher Education) Project (Brown, 1972; Miller and Prince, 1976). These efforts echoed the call, but with more tangible programs and implementation strategies, of earlier pioneers in the field such as Esther Lloyd-Jones ([1934] 1986), Ralph Berdie ([1966] 1983), and E. G. Williamson ([1967] 1986). If the student affairs field takes this broader mission seriously, then student affairs practitioners must systematically assess the effects on students of both their support and educational services and programs.

The creation of standards and guidelines by the Council for the Advancement of Standards for Student Services/Development Programs ([CAS] 1986) can be interpreted as a direct response to the move toward professionalism. And, of course, standards have no meaning unless there are efforts to determine whether programs and services meet or fulfill their criteria. These developments in the student affairs field were mirrored by similar initiatives in the academic arena through what has become known as the outcomes assessment or institutional effectiveness movement. Nichols (1989, p. 8) maintains that four common components exist for determining the institutional effectiveness or outcomes assessment: "(1) a clear statement of institutional purpose, mission, goals, or objectives, (2) identification of intended departmental/programmatic outcomes or objectives supporting accomplishment of the institutional statement of purpose, (3) establishment of effective means for assessment of the extent to which departmental/programmatic outcomes or objectives have been accomplished, [and] (4) utilization of assessment results to improve or change institutional, programmatic, or departmental intentions or operations."

In this chapter we define outcomes assessment within the context of student affairs and present a model for conceptualizing the enterprise. The use of *CAS Standards and Guidelines* (CAS, 1986) in outcomes assessment is discussed, and the methodological issues inherent in outcomes assessment are addressed. Finally, a selection of instruments and other measurement techniques that may be useful in outcomes assessment are presented.

Defining Outcomes Assessment

On the surface outcomes assessment addresses an important, but simple, question: What do students gain from attending college? For many years, however, higher education has tended to beg the question by talking about resources rather than outcomes (Astin, 1985). "Quality" education from the resource perspective results from being highly selective in admissions, employing a faculty with impressive academic credentials, maintaining low student-teacher ratios, expending large amounts of money on library materials, attracting sizable research grants, and having large endowments or substantial public financial support.

Although not unrelated to resources, outcomes assessment requires a redirection of the above question: How do students change as a result of attending college? Even more specifically, what do students get out of attending a particular college? The latter question, however, cannot be answered without first addressing the question, How should students change (or how do we intend for students to change) as a result of attending this particular institution?

Terenzini (1989, p. 648) proposed a taxonomic model (Figure 1) of approaches to assessment, which, with minor changes, can be useful in understanding outcomes assessment strategies and concerns in student affairs. The three dimensions of the cube address (1) the object of assessment, or the what; (2) the purpose of assessment, or the why; and (3) the level of assessment, or the who. All good assessment programs must carefully consider each of these dimensions and understand the implications of the decisions that must be made about each.

Figure 1. Taxonomy of Outcomes Assessment Approaches for Student Affairs

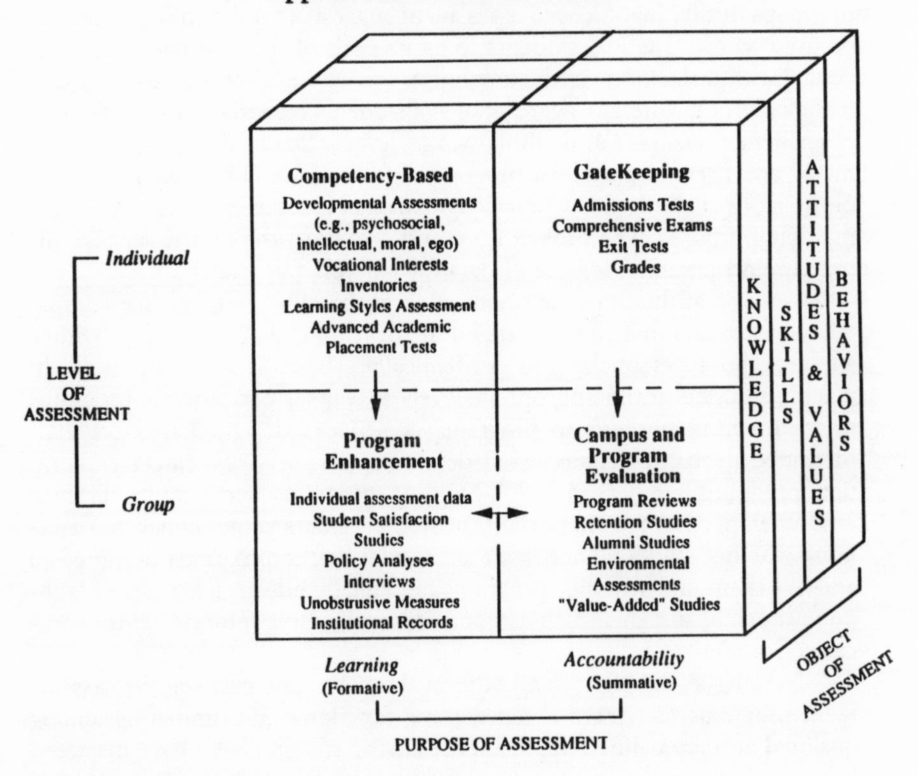

Source: Terenzini, 1989, p. 648. Reprinted by permission.

This model utilizes the topology of assessment outcomes proposed by Ewell (1983, 1985, 1987) to classify the object of assessment, which includes (1) depth and breadth of knowledge, (2) skills (academically related, career related, and interpersonal), (3) attitudes and values, and (4) behaviors (which include what students do while enrolled and after graduation).

The purposes of assessment fall into two broad, somewhat overlapping categories: (1) enhancement of learning and development and (2) accountability. These classifications can also be thought of as serving formative and summative purposes. Formative assessments provide information that is useful in determining effectiveness, or how well a program is functioning as the process continues, which allows for midcourse changes and corrections. Summative assessments provide information that can lead to making decisions about usefulness or merit of programs and interventions, cost-effectiveness, and actual effects.

The level of assessment determines whether the focus is on individuals or groups. Individual-focused assessment suggests that the information will be used with individual students to assist each of them in becoming successful within the limits of the institution's structure. Group-focused assessment looks at meaningful aggregations of students on variables such as place of residence, sex, race and ethnicity, age, level of academic skills, academic major, and users of particular programs and services. Other salient features of the model include the acknowledgment that assessment data often serve multiple purposes. The broken lines and arrows in the model suggest this overlap and potential for use of data for multiple purposes.

Looking at the upper-left-hand side of the cube, one can see competency-based data that concentrate on the developmental status of individual students, both personally and academically. These data can be useful in placing students at the appropriate levels of courses or academic programs or in directing students to programs or services designed to meet their identified needs, for example, academic support services, career exploration programs, or personal skill-building programs and groups. From a group perspective, it is important for student affairs professionals to determine whether students' needs are being met by the programs designed to address them and whether programs are equally effective for various subpopulations of students, such as nontraditional, ethnic minority, and handicapped students.

Looking at the right-hand side of the cube, one can see that assessment programs can serve a gatekeeping function—discriminating among qualified and unqualified applicants or among students who have mastered basic academic skills, such as in writing, at the end of one or two years of study or who have adequate knowledge in the academic major at graduation. The gatekeeping function is generally the province of academic affairs; student affairs generally becomes involved only in implementation of policies through admissions or the registrar's office. Student affairs is much more involved in determining program effectiveness and assessing the overall environmental climate of the institution and its influence on student retention and satisfaction (the lower-right-hand side of the cube).

Determining What to Assess

Over a half-century ago, Kurt Lewin (1935) proposed a comprehensive, person-environment interaction model for understanding human behavior and personality development. His simple formula $B = f(P, E)$, or behavior (B) is a function (f) of person (P) and environment (E) interaction, still has powerful explanatory significance for higher education today. Broadly speaking, the CAS (1986) standards for research and evaluation follow this interactionist approach by focusing on two primary areas of emphasis: (1) students and their development (person) and (2) programs/services and their effectiveness (environment). At the core of these two areas are two parallel questions: How well does the institution educate its students? What practices produce institutional effectiveness? Through these powerful, global questions, the standards provide a framework for determining what to assess in a comprehensive outcomes assessment effort.

Specifically, the CAS standards specify or imply a series of areas for study in each of the two broad emphases: person and environment. Person or individual developmental domains include description of students in terms of demographic and developmental characteristics, and personal behavior, needs assessment (for programming purposes), developmental changes (across a wide range of dimensions, such as career, intellectual, social/emotional, moral, spiritual, and physical), and student satisfaction. Environmental factors include evaluation of programs/services with respect to particular goals and objectives, identification of environmental conditions that inhibit or foster learning, and description of specific kinds of learning opportunities both in and (especially) outside of the classroom.

While not all of these lines of inquiry relate directly to student outcomes, the CAS standards appropriately recognize that an understanding of student learning outcomes requires analysis of both the person and the environment from multiple perspectives. Moreover, although this range represents an ideal comprehensive effort, institutions should vary in their specific emphases and approaches and will have to make decisions about how best to phase in their own particular versions of an assessment program.

Specifically with respect to student outcomes, the standards reflect a growing synthesis of work done over the years on taxonomies of educational outcomes. The Terenzini model (see Figure 1) focuses on knowledge, skills, attitudes and values, and behavior (the latter of which is often a manifestation of the previous three areas, but also often a separate line of inquiry). The Advisory Committee to the College Outcomes Evaluation Project (1987), in an adaptation of work done for the National Center for Higher Education Management Systems (NCHEMS) (Lenning, 1979), described a somewhat similar organizational taxonomy: academic performance, personal development, student experience (involvement, satisfaction), and postcollege activities, success, and satisfaction. Despite differences in component labels, these approaches are relatively congruent with the specifics defined in most of the functional area CAS standards. At least at this broad, conceptual level, it would be fair to say that higher education knows what it needs to assess in terms of student outcomes.

Crucial Role of Institutional Mission and Objectives. For better or worse, however, an assessment program cannot be done effectively from such a broad, generic perspective; it must be individualized and tailored to a specific institutional setting. Thus, as Jacobi, Astin, and Ayala (1987) noted, a coherent philosophy of institutional mission is fundamental to any assessment effort because a clear mission should drive the institution's conception of what constitutes effective performance in that context.

The Southern Association of Colleges and Schools ([SACS] 1989–1990) has built this foundation into its criteria for accreditation by requiring two steps prior to any actual assessment effort: (1) the establishment of a clearly defined purpose appropriate to collegiate education and (2) the formulation of educational goals consistent with the institution's purpose. Without these prior steps, assessment programs are likely to be unfocused at best and marginal in their potential impact on the institution.

Unfortunately, it is much easier to support the need for a coherent and clearly defined mission statement than it is to actually agree on what that statement should be. As Hartle (1985, p. 15) observed, "The central problem is that measuring educational achievement may well require more agreement about the ends and means of a higher education than we have at most institutions." Partly as a result of this lack of consensus, a typical mission statement tends to be as vague and generic as possible, thus ensuring that no one can possibly disagree with it (if indeed they can even understand it!). SACS (1989–1990, p. 7) notes this problem, insisting that "significantly greater clarity and specificity in statements will likely be needed" if the assessment of outcomes and institutional effectiveness is to have any real chance for success.

Clarifying an Institutional Mission Statement: A Case Study. One illustrative example of the process of defining and operationalizing an institutional mission statement comes from Longwood College in Virginia. Since 1983 the student affairs division at Longwood College, a medium-sized (approximately three thousand undergraduates), public, comprehensive college, has been engaged in a series of interventions designed to help students begin to understand the concept of involvement and its potential benefits for learning and development. Initial efforts were focused on the definition and assessment of college-wide developmental learning goals (Gorski, Moore, Strohm, and Taylor, 1985; Moore, 1988a), which fit within the institution's goals. More recently, the project has broadened to include an innovative effort to "map" the "hidden curriculum" of the college, that is, to articulate in some detail the significant learning opportunities existing for students in the college environment outside of the formal classroom setting.

A committee composed of professionals from across the various student affairs departments worked for two years in designing the project, gathering and compiling information and distilling the information gleaned into a set of "learning maps," one for each of the individual student affairs offices. The map data were gathered through written questionnaires and follow-up conversations with directors and other professional staff members, addressing the following questions: What is the mission of your agency/function? What specific educational themes or opportunities do you offer students? What are the significant learning outcomes that students can achieve through your area? How are those outcomes connected to the overall student learning goals defined by the college?

Structured worksheets were used to help focus the responses to these broad questions, and extended discussions were held with individual directors to clarify their thinking. As an example, the Student Union map defined four major domains of learning: leadership, resource management, facilities operation, and lifelong learning and recreation. Specific learning opportunities were identified and goals were enumerated in terms of attitudes, skills, and knowledge. For example, the learning opportunities associated with leadership development in the union included the Student Union Board, Leadership Education Team, and Leadership Conference—all activities or groups sponsored by or advised by the Student Union office. One of the attitude goals for that domain was "gain improved self-image and increased self-confidence"; a skill goal was "develop skills in interpersonal communication, delegation, problem solving, goal setting, and organizational politics"; and a knowledge goal was "understand styles of leadership and how complex organizations function." (Additional information about opportunities maps can be obtained from the Vice-President for Student Affairs, Longwood College, Farmville, Virginia 23901.)

The primary purpose of this mapping project was to produce materials that could be used to help students understand more clearly the involvement and learning opportunities that exist throughout the college environment. An unanticipated benefit of the project, however, was the opportunity for the professional staff members of student affairs to clarify their missions and provide direction for evaluating programs and services in terms of specific student behaviors. This project increased both the focus on and the understanding of the learning outcomes available to students through the various student affairs functional areas. Work continues in designing effective tools for disseminating this information to students. Maps have the potential for serving as starting points for a more precise assessment of student learning in the cocurriculum, as well as a clearer conceptualization of the overall college environment.

Designing Ways to Assess Outcomes

Once reasonable closure has been reached in terms of deciding which of the outcomes congruent with the institution's goals are to be assessed within the student affairs division, issues of evaluation design must be addressed. Hanson (1988) identified a number of thorny problems that must be considered when planning assessment designs, including the following.

How Students Change Over Time. Adequate outcomes assessment needs to take into account not only those variables that can be expected to change during the course of students' academic careers but also those concerned with how change occurs. Most theories of student development maintain that both qualitative and quantitative changes occur as students move through the stages and developmental sequences of the life cycle. An understanding of the major theories of human development, such as those of Perry (1970), Chickering (1969), Loevinger (1976), Super (1983), Kohlberg (1984), Belenky, Clinchy, Goldberger, and Tarule (1986), and Gilligan (1982, 1986), are necessary in order to inform student affairs evaluators about what to look for (including differences related to gender, ethnicity, or age) and when would be the most advantageous times to take measurements. For instance, many areas of development, such as intellectual or moral development, change rather slowly, and as a consequence data collection at short intervals is pointless and may even be misleading. Also, as Hanson (1988) pointed out, data collection at the freshman and senior years may mask changes that occurred during the sophomore and junior years and are not evident during the senior year. For example, students in nontechnical or nonscientific fields who take mathematics early in their academic careers may show substantial gains in knowledge of mathematics between the freshman and sophomore years, but by the end of the senior year they may not score any higher than they did as freshman on a mathematics achievement measure. Development seldom moves in a straight line and regression is a definite possibility.

Global Versus Specific Effects. Traditionally, when measuring outcomes, it has been assumed that college attendance has a global effect on students, that is, affects all students in the same way. Such an assumption is undermined by what is known from both research and common sense, that is, differences in personality, background, abilities, learning styles, and motivation—to name only a few variables—affect students' educational experiences differentially. College produces specific effects (Hanson, 1988), that is, effects that are contingent on individual characteristics and the extent or intensity of both the curricular and cocurricular activities in which students participate. Astin's (1985) involvement theory emphasizes the old aphorism "you get out of something what you put into it." Adequate outcomes assessment, then, must take into account initial differences in the student population and must account for both the extent and the intensity of involvement in programs, activities, and services.

Direct Versus Indirect Effects. It is tempting to try to assess the effects of programs and services immediately after exposure. Unfortunately, much of what is done in student affairs to influence the development of students may not produce evidence of direct effects. For instance, Pascarella, Terenzini, and Wolfle (1986) found that a pre-enrollment orientation program produced no direct effect on retention rate at the end of the first year. There were, however, indirect effects attributable to the orientation program because it affected students' social integration into the institution, which in turn affected their retention.

Traditionally, student affairs has been concerned about the learning climate and social environment in which students live. The main responsibility of monitoring and structuring many of the dominate environmental features of a campus often falls under the province of student affairs. Considerable research (Moos, 1979; Pace, 1979; Huebner, 1989; Huebner and Lawson, 1990) has documented that how students experience the institution affects their productivity, satisfaction, achievement, personal development, and health. Generally, however, it is not possible to establish a one-to-one correspondence between particular environmental features and certain student behaviors. The effects of many salient environmental features, increasingly referred to as institutional culture (Kuh, Whitt, and Shedd, 1987; Kuh and Whitt, 1988; Kuh, 1989), are pervasive and often indirect.

Psychometric Problems in Measuring Change. A principal difficulty in measuring change is attributable to the assessment instruments available. Most instruments, unless they are specifically designed to measure development, assess static traits that have a high degree of stability over time. As a consequence, these instruments may not be capable of detecting the changes associated with college attendance (Hanson, 1982, 1988). "To the extent that an assessment instrument is a static test and there is a high correlation across two points in time, there will be lower reliability of the change scores for individuals" (Hanson, 1988, p. 57). There is also a statistical problem in assessing change in groups. "In comparison of two groups over time, with existing first-time differences measured, the group that scores lower automatically shows greater change when measured the second time. This change has nothing to do with developmental growth or learning; again, it is an artifact of the measurement process" (Hanson, 1988, p. 58).

Analysis of Change Data. A popular, but flawed, approach to assessing outcomes has been to calculate gain scores, that is, the differences between initial scores on a measure and scores after the intervention or the passage of one or more academic terms, to determine the effects of programs or to estimate developmental change. There are many problems, however, with these approaches, including unreliability of results and a negative correlation with students' initial statuses (Linn, 1981; Banta, Lambert, Pike, Schmidhammer, and Schneider, 1987). More appropriate means of analysis may be residual gain scores, multiple correlation techniques, regression analysis, causal modeling (which can help to explain both direct and indirect effects), and hierarchical linear analysis (Hanson, 1988).

Evaluation Designs

There traditionally have been two basic approaches to evaluation design in outcomes assessment: cross-sectional and longitudinal. Cross-sectional research entails collecting data at one point in time from representatives of different target populations, for example, freshmen and seniors. Differences between the performances of these two groups are taken as indications of the effects of an intervention or of the college experience. This approach is particularly attractive because it requires only one data collection point. There are major methodological problems, however, associated with cross-sectional studies.

Cross-Sectional Designs. Limitations of cross-sectional designs for determining outcomes are directly linked to sampling problems. Researchers must be concerned about whether the individuals selected for study are truly representative of the target populations, for example, freshmen and seniors. Even if samples accurately reflect important variables in the populations, there is an additional problem in looking at differences between the two cohorts. All colleges have attrition between the freshman and senior years. In other words, only students who remain enrolled for a full course of study will be represented in the senior sample, and it is reasonable to suppose that there are important differences between those who stay until graduation and those who do not. As Terenzini (1989) noted, seniors as a group are likely to have higher aptitude and achievement records and a greater commitment to college than those who drop out. Other concerns include changes that might have occurred over the four-year period, such as changes in admissions standards, availability of financial aid funds, recruiting strategies, and social or historical events (for example, the emergence of AIDS and its effect on sexual practices or the protest over the war in Vietnam during an earlier time). Cross-sectional designs generally have the problem of comparing nonequivalent groups and require adjustments statistically to control for differences in variables such as age, academic ability, ethnicity, sex, and some personality characteristics.

Longitudinal Designs. Following a single group of students from matriculation to graduation in a longitudinal study avoids some of the difficulties inherent to cross-sectional designs; nonetheless, there are difficulties in this approach as well: (1) It is difficult to keep track of students over a period of years. Attrition of participants in longitudinal studies is a major problem that requires a considerable expenditure of time, energy, and money to combat. (2) There is need for a control group with which to make comparisons. It is nearly impossible, for example, to gather comparable data from a sample of high school graduates who did not attend college over a four-year period. (3) Because of the high mortality rate among research participants, longitudinal studies require large initial samples, making them rather expensive to conduct. (4) Due to the need to wait a number of years during data collection, longitudinal studies do not produce data in as timely a fashion as may be needed for accountability purposes. (5) Because of the somewhat transient nature of employment in higher education, it is often difficult to assemble a research/assessment staff that will be able to follow longitudinal studies through to completion.

Other Research Design Concerns. No matter whether cross-sectional or longitudinal designs are used, there are other important concerns to consider when creating an outcomes assessment plan. Because we know that all students are not alike, it is necessary to ensure that students with particular characteristics are present in sufficient number to allow for analyses of possible interaction effects. For example, potential moderator variables such as race, sex, age, socioeconomic background, academic major, academic achievement, personality type, and sexual orientation—that is, factors that are measured, manipulated, or observed in order to determine how they modify or affect the relationship between the independent variable and the outcomes measure—may be important in studies of educational outcomes. With the addition of each possible moderator variable, however, the number of students required in the study rises proportionally.

As Erwin (1989, 1990) has pointed out, there are important practical decisions to be made when deciding on assessment designs. For instance, what mechanisms are available for collecting data? (Can/will the institution mandate participation? If participation is mandatory, will disgruntled students take the task seriously? Will instructional/class time be used to collect data?) For practical reasons, assessment instruments must be relatively short and easy to administer and score. Unfortunately, those requirements present crucial challenges in terms of instrument reliability and validity. Finally, a responsive and thorough information management system is essential for adequate outcomes assessment to exist. As Kalsbeek (1989, p. 509) has noted, "A concerted information management effort may be the most effective of all professional roles in achieving such broad institutional objectives as enhancing the quality of student life, promoting student development in and out of the classroom, maximizing student involvement, responding to the diversity of learners in today's classrooms, and demonstrating educational and developmental outcomes."

Measurement Tools and Strategies

As mentioned earlier, outcomes in the overall person/environment arena that address these two primary focus areas in the CAS standards can be broadly categorized as academic performance, developmental changes, student experiences, and postcollege activities. In the following sections, we present a brief overview of some of the major measurement techniques and tools available in each of these areas.

Academic Performance. The most obvious surface markers in this area include current grading practices (GPA or grade point average) and retention/persistence information. Assessment of basic knowledge/competence can be done through, among others, the American College Testing Program (ACT), the Scholastic Aptitude Test, the ACT-COMP battery of tests, the relatively new Educational Testing Service (ETS) Academic Profile measures for specific disciplines, the Graduate Record Examination, and various specialized professional tests (for example, the National Teachers' Examination for prospective teachers). Northeast Missouri State University

(NMSU) is a primary example of an institution with an emphasis on this kind of standardized approach to assessment (NMSU, 1982). The state of Tennessee has mandated the use of the ACT-COMP for assessment purposes throughout its higher education system (Banta, 1988). Other institutions and states, dissatisfied with the limitations of such instruments as the ACT-COMP and the ETS Academic Profile, are designing their own local assessment tools tailored to the specifics of their own curricula. If we refer to the assessment model presented earlier (see Figure 1), these kinds of instruments serve gatekeeping functions and may be useful in program evaluation if used in pre-post designs.

Developmental Changes. The potential developmental impact of college occurs across a wide range of dimensions, including intellectual/cognitive, emotional/social, career, and personal (for example, spiritual and physical). In the intellectual domain, numerous approaches exist, from a traditional focus on basic critical thinking skills (the two best-known measures being the Watson-Glaser Critical Thinking Appraisal (Watson and Glaser, 1980) and the Cornell Test of Critical Thinking (Ennis and Millman, 1985), but there are several other alternatives that are more explicitly developmental measures (see Kurfiss, 1988, for a review). The Perry (1970) scheme is probably the most prominent of the developmental models in this area, with major instruments including the Measure of Intellectual Development (Knefelkamp, 1974; Moore, 1988b; Widick, 1975), the Measure of Epistemological Reflection (Baxter Magolda and Porterfield, 1988), and the Learning Environment Preferences (Moore, 1989). Reflective Judgment (RJ) (Kitchener and King, 1990) is a related but broader and less focused cognitive model, measured by the Reflective Judgment Interview. Moral development and moral judgment, while not as directly related to cognitive complexity as the Perry scheme or RJ, nevertheless constitute a significant dimension for many educational institutions and are measured most commonly by Rest's (1979) Defining Issues Test, Kohlberg's Moral Judgment Interview (Colby, Kohlberg, Speicher, Hewer, Candee, Gibbs, and Power, 1987), and, more recently, Gilligan's Voice Interviews (Gilligan, 1982, 1986). (These measurement approaches clearly fit on the left-hand side of the assessment model depicted in Figure 1.)

In the career domain, a wide variety of instruments exist with varying emphases. Some measures, such as the Strong Vocational Interest Inventory (Strong, Hansen, and Campbell, 1988), Vocational Preference Inventory (Holland, 1975), and Myers-Briggs Type Indicator (Myers and McCaulley, 1985), focus on interest patterns and personality differences across people, disciplines, and careers. These measures, while not outcome-oriented, can still be useful in providing students with significant career-related feedback in the assessment process. Other career-related measures focus on career maturity, career developmental issues, and the quality and certainty of career decision-making—for example, the Career Maturity Inventory (Crites, 1973),

Career Decision Scale (Osipow, 1987), My Vocational Situation (Holland, Daiger, and Power, 1989), and Career Development Inventory (CDI) (Super, Thompson, Lindeman, Jordan, and Myers, 1981). The career domain is problematic, however, because many of the instruments measure static traits, with the exception of the CDI, which is developmental in approach, and, therefore, are not sensitive to developmental change.

In the emotional/social arena, there are a few traditional psychological measures available, such as the Omnibus Personality Inventory (Heist and Yonge, 1968), Study of Values (Allport, Vernon, and Lindzey, 1970), and Values Sale (Super and Neville, 1981), but the most widely used developmental instrument for the past several years has been the Student Developmental Task Inventory (Winston, Miller, and Prince, 1979), revised and now known as the Student Developmental Task and Lifestyle Inventory (Winston, Miller, and Prince, 1987). This instrument assesses a number of different aspects of Chickering's (1969) vector model of psychosocial development in college students (including management of emotions, mature interpersonal relationships, and sense of purpose), along with some new scales focusing on intimacy and healthy lifestyle issues. More recently, researchers at the University of Iowa have made available a series of instruments (collectively called the Iowa Student Development Inventories) that measure specific developmental tasks described by Chickering's model, for example, an identity scale and a developing-a-sense-of-purpose scale (Hood, 1986). (See Miller and Winston, 1990, for brief descriptions of the psychosocial measures.)

Finally, in the personal arena, few formal measurement options exist for areas like spiritual or physical development, despite their importance in a holistic approach to lifelong education. There is some work in the area of wellness, for example, the Lifestyle Assessment Questionnaire (Elsenrath, Hettler, and Leafgren, 1988), and Fowler's (1981) work in faith development has produced an intensive interview protocol, but little has been done thus far to integrate either dimension into any significant outcome assessment efforts. (The instruments identified in the previous two sections clearly fall on the left-hand side of the assessment model depicted in Figure 1.)

Student Experiences. Because participation in most student-affairs-sponsored programs and services is voluntary, it is necessary to establish which are actually used by students and the extent of their involvement in the total college experience. The following list identifies instruments or tools that can be used in this aspect of outcomes assessment (that is, those fitting in the lower right-hand quadrant of the assessment model depicted in Figure 1): College Student Experiences Questionnaire (Pace, 1987), ACT Student Opinion Surveys (ACT, 1981), University Residence Environment Scales (Moos and Gerst, 1974), Extracurricular Involvement Inventory (Winston and Massaro, 1987), Institutional Functioning Inventory (Peterson, Centra, Hartnett, and Linn, 1970), College Student Satisfaction Questionnaire (Betz and Menke, 1971), locally-designed satisfaction surveys, exit interviews with withdrawing/graduating students, campus culture audit (Kuh and Whitt, 1988), specific program and service evaluation efforts, Academic and Social Integration Scale (Pascarella and Terenzini, 1978), and NCHEMS/College Board Student Outcomes Information Services (Ewell, 1983).

Post-College Activities. There are few commercially available instruments for assessing postcollege activities. Such followups are particularly difficult because of the mobility of recent graduates as they move across the country in pursuit of career advancement. The following are typical approaches to addressing postcollege activities: alumni surveys on satisfaction and success, employment history detailing required skills and salary levels, professional and civic activities, and recognition and awards.

Tracking Student Involvement: An Example

A crucial concern in attempting to assess the impact of student affairs programs and services is simply the determination of which students actually participated or sought assistance. Prince George's Community College in Largo, Maryland, has been collecting student involvement data for over a decade. At all on-campus events, individual students are requested to sign in on demographic sheets by providing name and social security number. This information is later relayed to computer processing, and reports are generated periodically throughout the year based on the student profiles drawn from the data banks maintained by the institution.

The college is then able to track overall attendance levels at various types of programs, as well as identify involvement patterns of individual students. For example, in addition to being able to review program attendance by a variety of student subgroups categories (such as age, ethnic background, accumulated hours, or program of study), the college can review how well student leaders and other students who are highly involved with campus activities perform academically. These data also allow the college to address the age-old question in student affairs: If one hundred students participated in ten programs, is it the same ten students attending ten programs, or did one hundred different students attend the ten programs? This information can also be extremely useful for comprehensive program planning through the campus community.

Much of the demographic information at Prince George's is currently collected by hand, although the data are processed and analyzed by computer. It seems that it would be relatively inexpensive and feasible to create a completely computerized system by affixing bar codes to student ID cards (a practice already common on many campuses to facilitate use of library materials). An optical scanner could then read the codes quickly, thereby creating a minimum of inconvenience for student participants.

There are two issues, however, that must be faced when using such a tracking system: (1) It is feasible to gather such data only when the event or service provided has controlled access. For large-scale, outdoor events, it may not be possible to control access. Also, informal contacts, such as occur at student organization meetings or unscheduled encounters between students and staff members, do not lend themselves to such a tracking system. (2) Student confidentiality and privacy also must be addressed. A system to protect the individual identities of program utilizers is essential. Otherwise, students may not seek the assistance they need because of fear of having their problems or concerns exposed to the public. A difficult transition period in winning student compliance on many campuses can be anticipated.

Once the system is well established, however, students (as they do at Prince George's) will accept it as part of the culture and will look for the optical scanners or sign-in sheets as they enter the door at events. Such a tracking system could well be promoted on the basis of its ability to help students document entries on developmental transcripts.

Standards and Outcomes Assessment: Double-Edged Sword?

Outcomes assessment and professional practical standards can function in a symbiotic relationship—each reinforcing and nurturing the other. Practice standards serve an important function for student affairs practitioners in that they outline minimum criteria of acceptable practice in most functional areas, criteria that have been used effectively to improve practices through planning and evaluation efforts. These objective, professionally endorsed statements have also been useful in arguing within institutions for resources and justifying the retention of programs—without appearing totally self-serving. This use of standards, however, is a double-edged sword. The standards clearly require that student affairs divisions carefully evaluate the effectiveness of the services and programs offered and investigate the effects or outcomes associated with them. If a student affairs division fails to institute effective, comprehensive outcomes assessment programs, it conspicuously falls short of the minimum CAS standards and probably forfeits the protection that standards potentially afford. A major obstacle to performing "good" outcomes assessment as related to student affairs is the lack of effective tracking systems. This problem must be solved if major progress is to be made in this area.

The standards provide a structure for comparing programs and services across functional areas and give guidance in focusing self-studies and long-term planning efforts. By emphasizing the importance of evaluating programs and services within the context of the institution's mission, there is protection against the "homogenization" of higher education or the trend of insisting that all colleges be the same. Outcomes assessment data, likewise, should be used in program evaluation and self-studies. Standards are virtually meaningless unless there is a systematic, ongoing outcomes assessment program.

On many campuses there are student affairs professionals who are much more knowledgeable and sophisticated in their understanding of the methodological issues inherent to outcomes assessment than are many of their colleagues on the faculty. The use of outcomes assessment efforts and data in addressing institutional evaluations is an endeavor in which student affairs staff could provide leadership and expertise to their institutions. By providing this service to institutions there can be many opportunities to introduce the values associated with the development of the "whole student" into the institutional consciousness.

References

Advisory Committee to the College Outcomes Evaluation Project. "Subcommittee Reports: Student Development/Post-Collegiate Activities and Student Learning." Unpublished manuscript, New Jersey Department of Higher Education, Trenton, 1987.

Allport, G. W., Vernon, P. E., and Lindzey, G. *Study of Values: A Scale for Measuring the Dominate Interests in Personality.* (3rd ed.) Chicago: Riverside, 1970.

American College Testing Program (ACT). *Student Opinion Survey.* Iowa City, Iowa: ACT, 1981.

Astin, A. W. *Achieving Educational Excellence: A Critical Assessment of Priorities and Practices in Higher Education.* San Francisco: Jossey-Bass, 1985.

Banta, T. W. "Assessment as an Instrument of Student Funding Policy." In T. W. Banta (ed.), *Implementing Outcomes Assessment: Promises and Perils.* New Directions for Institutional Research, no. 59. San Francisco: Jossey-Bass, 1988.

Banta, T. W., Lambert, W., Pike, G., Schmidhammer, J., and Schneider, J. "Estimated Student Score Gain on the ACT-COMP Exam: Valid Tool for Institutional Assessment?" Paper presented at the annual meetings of the American Educational Research Association, Washington, D.C., April 1987.

Baxter Magolda, M., and Porterfield, W. *Assessing Intellectual Development: The Link Between Theory and Practice.* Alexandria, Va.: American College Personnel Association, 1988.

Belenky, M. F., Clinchy, B. M., Goldberger, N. R., and Tarule, J. M. *Women's Ways of Knowing: The Development of Self, Voice, and Mind.* New York: Basic Books, 1986.

Berdie, R. F. "Student Personnel Work: Definition and Redefinition." In B. A. Belson and L. E. Fitzgerald (eds.), *Thus, We Spoke: ACPA-NAWDAC, 1958–1975.* Alexandria, Va.: American College Personnel Association, 1983. (Originally published 1966.)

Betz, E. L., and Menke, J. W. *College Student Satisfaction Questionnaire* (Form C). Cambridge, Iowa: Authors, 1971.

Brown, R. D. *Student Development in Tomorrow's Higher Education: A Return to the Academy.* Washington, D.C.: American College Personnel Association, 1972.

Chickering, A. W. *Education and Identity.* San Francisco: Jossey-Bass, 1969.

Colby, A., Kohlberg, L., Speicher, B., Hewer, A., Candee, D., Gibbs, J., and Power, C. *The Measurement of Moral Judgment.* Vol. 2: *Standard Issue Scoring Manual.* New York: Cambridge University Press, 1987.

Council for the Advancement of Standards for Student Services/Development Programs (CAS). *CAS Standards and Guidelines for Student Services/Development Programs.* Washington, D.C.: CAS, 1986.

Council of Student Personnel Associations (COSPA). *Student Development Services in Higher Education.* Washington, D.C.: COSPA, 1972.

Crites, J. O. *Career Maturity Inventory.* Monterey, Calif.: CTB/McGraw-Hill, 1973.

Elsenrath, D., Hettler, B., and Leafgren, F. *Lifestyle Assessment Questionnaire.* (5th ed.) Stevens Point, Wis.: National Wellness Institute, 1988.

Ennis, R. H., and Millman, J. *Cornell Tests of Critical Thinking.* Pacific Grove, Calif.: Midwest, 1985.

Erwin, T. D. "New Opportunities: How Student Affairs Can Contribute to Outcomes Assessment." In U. Delworth, G. R. Hanson, and Associates, *Student Services: A Handbook for the Profession.* (2nd ed.) San Francisco: Jossey-Bass, 1989.

Erwin, T. D. "Student Outcomes Assessment: An Institutional Perspective." In D. G. Creamer and Associates, *College Student Development: Theory and Practice for the 1990s.* Alexandria, Va.: American College Personnel Association, 1990.

Ewell, P. T. *Information on Student Outcomes: How to Get It and How to Use It.* Boulder, Colo.: National Center for Higher Education Management Systems, 1983. (ED 246 827)

Ewell, P. T. "Some Implications for Practice." In P. T. Ewell (ed.), *Assessing Educational Outcomes.* New Directions for Institutional Research, no. 47. San Francisco: Jossey-Bass, 1985.

Ewell, P. T. "Establishing a Campus-Based Assessment Program." In D. F. Halpern (ed.), *Student Outcomes Assessment: What Institutions Stand to Gain.* New Directions for Higher Education, no. 59. San Francisco: Jossey-Bass, 1987.

Fowler, J. *Stages of Faith.* New York: Harper & Row, 1981.

Gilligan, C. *In a Different Voice: Psychological Theory and Women's Development.* Cambridge, Mass.: Harvard University Press, 1982.

Gilligan, C. "Remapping Development: The Power of Divergent Data." In L. Cirillo and S. Wapner (eds.), *Value Presuppositions in Theories of Human Development.* Hillsdale, N.J.: Erlbaum, 1986.

Gorski, B., Moore, W. S., Strohm, M., and Taylor, K. "Student Development: The Longwood Experience." *Bulletin of the Association of College Unions-International,* 1985, *53* (3), 21–25.

Hanson, G. R. "Critical Issues in the Assessment of Student Development." In G. R. Hanson (ed.), *Measuring Student Development.* New Directions for Student Services, no. 20. San Francisco: Jossey-Bass, 1982.

Hanson, G. R. "Critical Issues in the Assessment of Value Added in Education." In T. W. Banta (ed.), *Implementing Outcomes Assessment: Promise and Perils.* New Directions for Institutional Research, no. 59. San Francisco: Jossey-Bass, 1988.

Hartle, T. "The Growing Interest in Measuring the Educational Achievement of College Students." In C. Adelman (ed.), *Assessment in American Higher Education: Issues and Contexts.* Washington, D.C.: U.S. Office of Educational Research and Improvement, 1985.

Heist, P., and Yonge, G. *Omnibus Personality Inventory.* New York: Psychological Corporation, 1968.

Holland, J. L. *Vocational Preference Inventory.* Palo Alto, Calif.: Consulting Psychologists Press, 1975.

Holland, J. L., Daiger, D., and Power, P. G. *My Vocational Situation.* Palo Alto, Calif.: Consulting Psychologists Press, 1989.

Hood, A. B. (ed.). *The Iowa Student Development Inventories.* Iowa City, Iowa: Hitech Press, 1986.

Huebner, L. A. "Interaction of Student and Campus." In U. Delworth, G. R. Hanson, and Associates, *Student Services: A Handbook for the Profession.* (2nd ed.) San Francisco: Jossey-Bass, 1989.

Huebner, L. A., and Lawson, J. M. "Understanding and Assessing College Environments." In D. G. Creamer and Associates, *College Student Development: Theory and Practice for the 1990s.* Alexandria, Va.: American College Personnel Association, 1990.

Jacobi, M., Astin, A. W., and Ayala, F., Jr. *College Student Outcomes Assessment.* ASHE-ERIC Higher Education Report No. 7. Washington, D.C.: Association for the Study of Higher Education, 1987.

Kalsbeek, D. H. "Managing Data and Information Resources." In U. Delworth, G. R. Hanson, and Associates, *Student Services: A Handbook for the Profession.* (2nd ed.) San Francisco: Jossey-Bass, 1989.

Kitchener, K. S., and King, P. M. "The Reflective Judgment Model: Transforming Assumptions About Knowing." In J. Mezirow and Associates (eds.), *Fostering Critical Reflection in Adulthood: A Guide to Transformative and Emancipatory Learning.* San Francisco: Jossey-Bass, 1990.

Knefelkamp, L. "Developmental Instruction: Fostering Intellectual and Personal Growth." Unpublished doctoral dissertation, Department of Educational Psychology, University of Minnesota, 1974.

Kohlberg, L. *Essays on Moral Development.* New York: Harper & Row, 1984.

Kuh, G. W. "Organizational Concepts and Influences." In U. Delworth, G. R. Hanson, and Associates, *Student Services: A Handbook for the Profession.* (2nd ed.) San Francisco: Jossey-Bass, 1989.

Kuh, G. W., and Whitt, E. J. *The Invisible Tapestry: Culture in American Colleges and Universities.* ASHE-ERIC Higher Education Report No. 1. Washington, D.C.: Association for the Study of Higher Education, 1988.

Kuh, G. W., Whitt, E. J., and Shedd, J. D. *Student Affairs Work 2001: A Paradigmatic Odyssey.* Alexandria, Va.: American College Personnel Association, 1987.

Kurfiss, J. *Critical Thinking: Theory, Research, Practice, and Possibilities.* ASHE-ERIC Higher Education Report No. 2. Washington, D.C.: Association for the Study of Higher Education, 1988.

Lenning, O. T. *The Outcomes Structure: An Overview and Procedure for Applying It in Postsecondary Educational Institutions.* Boulder, Colo.: National Center for Higher Educational Management Systems, 1979.

Lewin, K. *Dynamic Theory of Personality.* New York: McGraw-Hill, 1935.

Linn, R. L. "Measuring Pretest-Posttest Performance Changes." In R. Berk (ed.), *Educational Evaluation Methodology: The State of the Art.* Baltimore, Md.: Johns Hopkins University Press, 1981.

Lloyd-Jones, E. "Personnel Administration." In G. L. Saddlemire and A. L. Rentz (eds.), *Student Affairs: A Profession's Heritage.* Alexandria, Va.: American College Personnel Association, 1986. (Originally published 1934.)

Loevinger, J. *Ego Development: Conceptions and Theories.* San Francisco: Jossey-Bass, 1976.

Miller, T. K., and Prince, J. S. *The Future of Student Affairs: A Guide to Student Development for Tomorrow's Higher Education.* San Francisco: Jossey-Bass, 1976.

Miller, T. K., and Winston, R. B., Jr. "Assessing Development from a Psychosocial Perspective." In D. G. Creamer and Associates, *College Student Development: Theory and Practice for the 1990s.* Alexandria, Va.: American College Personnel Association, 1990.

Moore, W. S. "Assessing Student Development: The Longwood Experience." *Virginia Association of Student Personnel Administrators Interchange,* 1988a, *16* (2), 1–4.

Moore, W. S. *The Measure of Intellectual Development: An Instrument Manual.* Olympia, Wash.: Center for the Study of Intellectual Development, 1988b.

Moore, W. S. "The Learning Environment Preferences: Exploring the Construct Validity of an Objective Measure of the Perry Scheme of Intellectual Development." *Journal of College Student Development,* 1989, *30,* 504–514.

Moos, R. H. *Evaluating Educational Environments: Procedures, Measures, Findings, and Policy Implications.* San Francisco: Jossey-Bass, 1979.

Moos, R. H., and Gerst, M. *University Residence Environment Scale.* Palo Alto, Calif.: Consulting Psychologists Press, 1974.

Myers, I. B., and McCaulley, M. H. *Manual: A Guide to the Development and Use of the Myers-Briggs Type Indicator.* Palo Alto, Calif.: Consulting Psychologists Press, 1985.

Nichols, J. O. *Institutional Effectiveness and Outcomes Assessment Implementation on Campus: A Practitioner's Handbook.* New York: Agathon Press, 1989.

Northeast Missouri State University (NMSU). *Assessing the Quality of Undergraduate Education.* Kirksville, Mo.: NMSU, 1982.

Osipow, S. H. *Manual for the Career Decision Scale.* Odessa, Fla.: Psychological Assessment Resources, 1987.

Pace, C. R. *Measuring the Outcomes of College: Fifty Years of Findings and Recommendations for the Future.* San Francisco: Jossey-Bass, 1979.

Pace, C. R. *College Student Experiences Questionnaire: Test Manual and Norms.* Los Angeles: Center for the Study of Evaluation, University of California, 1987.

Pascarella, E. T., and Terenzini, P. T. "Student-Faculty Informal Relationships and Freshman Year Educational Outcomes." *Journal of Educational Research,* 1978, *71,* 183–189.

Pascarella, E. T., Terenzini, P. T., and Wolfle, L. "Orientation to College and Freshman Year Persistence/Withdrawal Decisions." *Journal of Higher Education,* 1986, *57,* 155–175.

Perry, W. G., Jr. *Forms of Intellectual and Ethical Development in the College Years: A Scheme.* New York: Holt, Rinehart & Winston, 1970.

Peterson, R., Centra, J., Hartnett, R., and Linn, R. *Institutional Functioning Inventory.* Princeton, N.J.: Educational Testing Service, 1970.

Rest, J. *Development in Judging Moral Issues.* Minneapolis: University of Minnesota Press, 1979.

Southern Association of Colleges and Schools (SACS). *Criteria for Accreditation: Commission on Colleges.* Atlanta, Ga.: SACS, 1989–1990.

Strong, E. K., Hansen, J. C., and Campbell, D. P. *Strong Vocational Interest Inventory.* Palo Alto, Calif.: Consulting Psychologists Press, 1988.

Super, D. E. "Assessment in Career Guidance: Toward Truly Developmental Counseling." *Personnel and Guidance Journal,* 1983, *61,* 555–562.

Super, D. E., and Neville, D. D. *Values Scale.* Palo Alto, Calif.: Consulting Psychologists Press, 1981.

Super, D. E., Thompson, A. S., Lindeman, R. H., Jordan, J. P., and Myers, R. A. *Career Development Inventory.* Palo Alto, Calif.: Consulting Psychologists Press, 1981.

Terenzini, P. T. "Assessment with Open Eyes: Pitfalls in Studying Student Outcomes." *Journal of Higher Education,* 1989, *60,* 644–665.

Watson, G., and Glaser, E. M. *Watson-Glaser Critical Thinking Appraisal.* San Antonio, Tex.: Psychological Corporation, 1980.

Widick, C. "An Evaluation of Developmental Instruction in a University Setting." Unpublished doctoral dissertation, Department of Educational Psychology, University of Minnesota, 1975.

Williamson, E. G. "Some Unresolved Problems in Student Personnel Work." In G. L. Saddlemire and A. L. Rentz (eds.), *Student Affairs: A Profession's Heritage.* Alexandria, Va.: American College Personnel Association, 1986. (Originally published in 1967.)

Winston, R. B., Jr., and Massaro, A. V. "Extracurricular Involvement Inventory: An Instrument for Assessing Intensity of Student Involvement." *Journal of College Student Personnel,* 1987, *28,* 169-175.

Winston, R. B., Jr., Miller, T. K., and Prince, J. S. *Student Developmental Task Inventory.* Athens, Ga.: Student Development Associates, 1979.

Winston, R. B., Jr., Miller, T. K., and Prince, J. S. *Student Developmental Task and Lifestyle Inventory.* Athens, Ga.: Student Development Associates, 1987.

Roger B. Winston, Jr., is professor in the Student Personnel in Higher Education Program at the University of Georgia, Athens.

William S. Moore is director of Student Outcomes Assessment, Washington State Board for Community College Education, Olympia.

CAS Standards and Guidelines has been used at a number of colleges and universities, where diverse creative methods of implementation have been employed to the benefit of the institutions.

Example Applications of CAS Standards and Guidelines

Joseph M. Marron

Five years have passed since the American College Testing Program, on behalf of the Council for the Advancement of Standards for Student Services/Development Programs (CAS), printed and mailed copies of *CAS Standards and Guidelines* (CAS, 1986) to each chief executive officer in institutions of higher education in the United States. Institutions have had sufficient time to examine and begin integrating these standards into their planning and evaluation processes. In addition, *CAS Self Assessment Guides* (Miller, Thomas, Looney, and Yerian, 1988) is available to assist practitioners in their planning for program improvement. Institutions of all sizes and types have begun to use the CAS standards and guidelines effectively to benefit their programs. In this chapter, examples of the uses of CAS standards and guidelines by a number of colleges and universities are presented, issues related to the use of standards are explored, and strengths and weaknesses in the present approaches are discussed. The seven institutional examples reported herein are among the most effective in their use of CAS standards and guidelines. The information presented was gained from telephone interviews with campus personnel who were instrumental in the application of CAS standards in their respective campus settings.

Syracuse University

In 1985, institutional services merged with student affairs to form the Division of Student Services at Syracuse University, Syracuse, New York (Mary Jo Custer, personal communication, November 28, 1989). The new vice-president for student services initiated a self-study for all departments under the umbrella of the division, and the decision was made to use *CAS Standards and Guidelines* (CAS, 1986) as the base document for the study.

The self-study was headed by an advisory board made up of four senior staff members in student services. This board set a one-year time line for the self-study, provided multiple copies of the CAS standards to all directors, and arranged for a review of standards with the advisory board.

Directors were encouraged to use a combination of CAS materials and other available standards. Residence life services used the CAS Standards and Guidelines for Housing and Residential Life (CAS, 1986) and the Association of College and University Housing Officers-International ([ACUHO-I] 1985) standards to complete its work. For some functional areas CAS standards were not available, and these functional areas looked to professional organizations for guidance. For example, the Food Service Department had the National Association of College and University Food Services (1986) standards to use as a reference. Some functional areas, such as student employment and business operations, had no reference points for standards. These functional areas were instructed to write a standards statement before they began their self-study, using the CAS format as a model. Most departments used *CAS Standards and Guidelines* as their primary reference document.

The advisory board, in accord with the consensus among higher education administrators, viewed *CAS Standards and Guidelines* as the only available comprehensive document for student affairs programs. During the self-study, staff meetings and retreats were held to familiarize division staff with the standards statements. The advisory board sponsored a midyear workshop to review the standards, answer questions, and outline the self-study process.

Results of the Syracuse student services self-study included the university winning a cost-reduction award for the project from the National Association of College and University Business Officers/United States Steel Federation. Within the division, new facilities were added to the Campus Recreation Center, including additional swimming, basketball, racquetball, and nautilus equipment; a second student union was built; one level of the original student center was renovated; an Office of Commuter Services and a Sanitation, Safety, and Recycling Office were established; new positions were created; current personnel were reorganized to increase efficiency; and most areas of the division, including the Research and Evaluation Office, received increases in funding.

When Syracuse University underwent an accreditation and reaffirmation review in 1988, the Division of Student Services used the self-study results extensively prior to the arrival of the visiting team from the Middle States accrediting body. The CAS-based self-study helped prepare Syracuse to deal with Middle States in functional areas such as recreational sports, day care, residence life, counseling, and special populations.

At Syracuse a favorable response for using the CAS materials and other standards was garnered from faculty, staff, and students who served on the self-study committees. Many faculty who took part in the process stated that the standards gave them a comprehensive academic perspective on student services for the first time. The advisory board provided a critical link in constituency acceptance of CAS standards and the self-study. The board assured division staff that if weaknesses were exposed, no staff member needed to worry about his or her position with the university.

The underlying theme of the CAS-based self-study was positive improvement. Professional staff members have reported direct outcomes from their efforts in the self-study and improvements in their departments. Mary Jo Custer (personal communication, November 28, 1989), assistant to the vice-president and chairperson of the advisory board, stated that "the machine is constantly being fined-tuned. Customers are being served with the help of CAS."

Notre Dame College

Alicia Finn (personal communication, November 21, 1989) went to Notre Dame College, Manchester, New Hampshire, to establish a counseling center. It was July 1986, only months after the publication of the CAS standards and guidelines, when she accepted the position. Soon after her arrival the vice-president informed her that the standards were available and might prove helpful to her in designing the college's counseling services. Finn studied the CAS document closely to ascertain if the Standards and Guidelines for Counseling Services (CAS, 1986) might have utility for her purposes. Despite an extensive professional background, she had not had the opportunity to create a new counseling center service and facility from the beginning. She decided that *CAS Standards and Guidelines* would make an excellent foundation document for the development of a new campus counseling services program.

Finn made the decision to follow the Standards and Guidelines for Counseling Services in establishing the center. The components of mission, program, organization and administration, human resources, funding, facilities, campus and community relations, ethics, and evaluation accurately reflected the needs of Notre Dame College at that critical juncture in project development. Program development decisions were largely made on the basis of the CAS standards, although sometimes these standards were exceeded. The guidelines provided great assistance in the development of policies and procedures for the center and in the formulation of a mission statement. Finn found an additional way to use the standards in building the center. After initial construction had begun, the college received a $10,000 grant to make the building accessible to persons with disabilities. Throughout the grant application, Finn had made reference not only to the

CAS counseling services standards but also to the standards concerned with disabled student services (CAS, 1986).

The support to establish Notre Dame's Counseling Center was unilateral. Originally, a faculty and staff committee urged the college to provide this service and the administration showed its trust in allowing Finn to decide how best to proceed. After four years of operation, faculty and administration are very enthusiastic about the center. A yearly student-life satisfaction survey gives it high marks.

After serving two years as director of the Counseling Center, Finn assumed the position of dean of student development. She made the decision to use the CAS standards on a division-wide basis. The process included introducing department directors to the CAS standards through formal staff meetings, asking directors to prepare verbal self-assessments of their departments based on the standards, meeting with each director to discuss department goals for the coming year, and developing budgets with the CAS standards as a guide. The timing was favorable for this process; both the directors and Finn appreciated *CAS Standards and Guidelines* as a staff development tool. The document proved to be a perfect introduction to the field for new professionals, while also serving as a revitalizing agent for the veteran professional staff members.

In two departments, campus ministry and student activities, student planning boards used the CAS standards. Finn viewed this student knowledge and use of the CAS standards as very healthy and beneficial to the institution. She also used the standards to form a peer review judicial system. The CAS standards and guidelines for judicial programs and services proved to be very beneficial in the review of the structure of this unit and allowed a further opportunity for student involvement with the standards.

The final application of the CAS standards at Notre Dame was with the President's Council. Finn shared the standards with her fellow senior administrators and stated to the council that the division used the standards as a backdrop to division planning. She also indicated to the President's Council that she wanted student affairs departments at the college to meet or exceed CAS standards for student affairs functional areas.

Use of the CAS standards in the student affairs planning process has been accepted by the various campus constituencies at Notre Dame. Tangible results include substantial reallocation of funds to and within the division, expansion of residence life programs and improvement in the quality of staff training, and increased division programming, particularly in the area of campus ministry.

What does the future hold for Notre Dame in terms of continued standards usage? Finn has decided that in the near future the division will embark on a planning process to devise one- and three-year plans for each department based on the CAS standards. She stated that "the CAS standards statement is the only document I know of that articulates the ideal structure and recommended guidelines for each student affairs department."

Sonoma State University

Rand Link (personal communication, November 20, 1989), dean of student affairs at Sonoma State University, Rohnert Park, California, identified four distinct applications of the CAS standards at his institution. He found *CAS Standards and Guidelines* to be to date the best and the most comprehensive effort put forth on professional standards development. He noted that the well-thought-out document also had the endorsement of over twenty professional associations in student affairs.

Application 1. Link first introduced the CAS standards to the university self-study committee prior to the university's reaccreditation visit by the Western Association of Schools and Colleges (WASC). The committee, made up of faculty and administrative staff, was informed about the CAS standards and guidelines and referred to them as needed, but actual usage was relatively minimal. Link informed the WASC executive director about the standards and they were shared with the visitation committee before they departed campus.

Application 2. The CAS standards were also used on the Sonoma campus in the area of planning in student affairs. Link suggested that the standards be used as a guide for goal setting in each department. The extent of the actual use of the standards was dependent on the individual department head. Link felt there was widespread but not universal usage of the standards by department directors. The standards, where appropriate, are now also being utilized as a touchstone in developing a five-year plan for student affairs at Sonoma, which is part of a campus-wide long-range planning effort.

Application 3. There is much more uniformity in Sonoma's third method of use than in the prior two applications. The CAS standards were used as a format for all annual reports within the Division of Student Affairs. Directors authored their reports using six of the CAS components: mission, program, human resources, funding, facilities, and evaluation. Program goals developed with the aid of the standards were also included in the annual reports. Particular emphasis was placed on evaluation in each report. Directors often used the CAS standards as one of their principal evaluation tools.

Application 4. The final application of the CAS standards at Sonoma reached well beyond the campus. The California State University Educational Support Services Master Plan Task Force, appointed by Chancellor W. Ann Reynolds, used the CAS standards extensively in its work. The final report, completed in May 1989, presented a long-range master plan in student services for the twenty campuses of the California State University

System (California State University, 1989). The Board of Trustees of the California State University formally adopted the plan in June 1989. The report called for universities to evaluate their student service programs every five years. Thirty recommendations were presented in the report, each to be implemented systemwide. The CAS standards served as one of the principal evaluation tools. In the areas of academic advising, career services, counseling services, disabled student services, learning assistance programs, residence life, and minority student programs, CAS functional area standards are the only recommended evaluation standards. With the Master Plan Task Force report carrying a full weight of influence, the CAS standards will soon be used on all twenty of the California campuses. Link anticipates that CAS standards applications will increase dramatically in the future.

Link was certain that the use of CAS standards will increase on his campus. H stated that he plans to develop an implementation strategy for the required five-year evaluation program and that the *CAS Self Assessment Guides* (Miller, Thomas, Looney, and Yerian, 1988) will be a major part of Sonoma's plan. Student affairs personnel have reported that the CAS standards are very useful; however, Link noted that he and several department heads found the standards to be limited in the area of minority affairs, precollege outreach programs, and counseling services. Specifically, his counseling staff evaluated their center using the American Psychological Association (1983) guidelines. This was not a criticism of the CAS standards, only an acknowledgment that in some areas there are more detailed sets of standards available.

Link found that it was difficult to substantively evaluate Sonoma State University's use of the CAS standards. Student affairs funding has not been increased and Sonoma is formula-funded on the basis of its student enrollment. The extent of knowledge of the standards among faculty members on campus is varied; Link hoped to increase campus knowledge in the future by introducing the CAS standards to the University Academic Senate through the Student Affairs Standing Committee. He believed that the use of the CAS standards was valuable for his university because positive reinforcement had accompanied each such effort. This positive reinforcement, coupled with Sonoma State University's Student Support Services Master Plan, served as his only method of evaluation.

Mississippi State University

Gerald Tice (personal communication, November 30, 1989), assistant to the vice-president for student affairs and director of housing and residence life at Mississippi State University, Mississippi State, provided feedback to CAS on early drafts of the CAS standards. He had reviewed the ACUHO-I (1985) standards and wanted to use CAS and ACUHO-I standards to undertake a self-study of his department. Tice's motivation to use the standards stemmed from his feeling that they provided an external mechanism for internal examination. These standards statements gave departments the ability to break from the routine of basing their evaluations only on past performance. Thus, the first example of student affairs standards usage on the campus of Mississippi State University was initiated.

Application 1. The self-study began with the formation of teams made up of student affairs professionals from both inside and outside the housing area. Each team was headed by an assistant director responsible for such functions as residence life, facilities, maintenance, administration, family housing, and conferences. Team leaders did not evaluate their own specialties, rather they examined areas where they were familiar with the operations but not directly involved in them. Sufficient time was allowed to study both the CAS and ACUHO-I standards as the participants were not familiar with the new documents. Upon completion of the individual studies, a formal report was presented, which included suggestions to bring the department into compliance with the standards.

Application 2. While the housing department self-study was taking place, a second application of the CAS standards emerged. Tice had informed Roy Ruby, vice-president for student affairs, that his department's project was underway. During the course of the discussion the decision was made to use the CAS standards on a division-wide basis. The CAS standards are now the basis for departmental self-evaluation each year. Each director and assistant director evaluates his or her respective area using the CAS standards as the criteria. A formal written report is submitted annually, indicating areas of compliance and noncompliance. Recommendations for improvement in the deficient areas is a major part of each report. Quality planning to comply with the standards is now very noticeable throughout the division, according to Tice.

Application 3. A third method of standards usage at Mississippi State is in the area of research. A research council was formed within the student affairs division that included 40 percent of the faculty. The council used *CAS Standards and Guidelines* to assist in goal setting. The group was given the document during the council's formation, and the standards emerged as the basis for most of the council's work. Specifically, the council designed methods that better enable the division to know its students. The research and evaluation section of the CAS standards has proved invaluable to the group. The additional seventeen functional areas provided a consistent resource to use as needed. The faculty who participated on the council had a keen interest in the student life aspects of the university. The standards helped to show them the rationale for many of the division's decisions, while increasing their knowledge about the student affairs division. The support for using the CAS standards on the research council continues to grow.

Strong support was also evident within the housing area from the first introduction of the CAS standards. Members of that department felt included in the decision to use the two sets of standards (CAS and ACUHO-I) and also in the creation of the process itself. They expressed a desire to lead the pack on standards usage. The standards were seen as tools that would assist in validating the programs and services of the housing unit not only for the vice-president but also for the rest of the division and the university at large.

Support grew slowly as the entire division became involved. Reaction varied by department and individual. While no active resistance was encountered, some hesitancy to fully embrace the standards was apparent. Now, after several years of using the standards, the division seems fully engaged in the process.

Plans for future use of the CAS standards are constantly changing at Mississippi State. The housing area plans to update continually its method of usage as needed. Tice stated that he hoped to create a model evaluation program that any student affairs division could use. He also intended to introduce *CAS Self Assessment Guides* (Miller, Thomas, Looney, and Yerian, 1988) to housing and the rest of the division when feasible. Tice concluded by stating, "I believe these benchmark publications will grow in importance throughout the coming decade and widespread usage will begin to occur on campuses across the country."

University of Wisconsin at LaCrosse

The graduate program in College Student Personnel at the University of Wisconsin, LaCrosse, was founded in 1968. Reid Horle (personal communication, November 17, 1989), dean of student development and coordinator of the College Student Personnel Program, decided in 1980 to ask a departmental curriculum committee to study course offerings and make recommendations for change. Only one major recommendation was made: Don't make any changes. The program continued for another three years until Horle again asked the curriculum committee to examine the structure of the program.

The publication *CAS Standards and Guidelines* in May 1986 coincided with the study of the College Student Personnel Program at LaCrosse. Horle was able to specifically point out the Preparation Standards and Guidelines at the Master's Degree Level for Student Services/Development Professionals in Postsecondary Education (CAS, 1986) to the committee. Unlike 1980, some serious recommendations to change the curriculum were adopted. The CAS preparation standards served as the basis for these revisions. The revised thirty-six semester-hours program had content taken directly from the standards, including the courses Human and Student Development Theory, Higher Education and the Student Personnel Function, College Students and Their Environment, Student Development and

Promotion: Theory and Application, Organization Theory and Behavior, Administration in Higher Education, Current Theories and Application of Career Development, and Research and Evaluation in College Student Personnel, as well as Internships and Practica.

Students can complete the program in two years if enrolled on a full-time basis. Graduate assistantship opportunities have improved considerably, and internship and practica experiences have been expanded to include two other institutions, giving students the opportunity to obtain practical experience in small private liberal arts and two-year vocational/technical college settings, as well as in the university setting.

The resulting changes in the college student personnel curriculum had strong support, although formal evaluation of program changes will be difficult. The fall 1989 class was the third class to begin the new program; the first class graduated in 1989. While it may be several years before a formal evaluation process can validate the program's success, consensus among the administration, faculty, student development practitioners, alumni, and students is that the curriculum based on the CAS preparation standards will prove to be strong, vibrant, and capable of attracting quality students.

Adrian College

Approximately twelve hundred students attend Adrian College, Adrian, Michigan. Robert Turek (personal communication, November 28, 1989) reported that this small, private, liberal arts college used the CAS standards and guidelines in several ways to enhance the quality of the programs within the Division of Student Affairs and, ultimately, the lives of its students. Turek, vice-president and dean for student affairs, along with a former colleague, initiated discussion about the CAS standards on the Adrian campus soon after their publication. Those discussions evolved into an annual program of CAS-oriented activities and evaluations.

Turek reported that senior student affairs staff members in the division meet formally with him to review the CAS standards on an annual basis. He also met with staff department heads outside of the division, but whose functional areas are incorporated within the CAS standards, to introduce the standards to them. The process was designed for department heads and staff members (1) to develop annual reports or reviews based on the CAS standards used during the previous academic year and (2) to use the CAS standards and guidelines to set goals and objectives for the coming year. These department goals and objectives are also used to aid the vice-president and the directors in setting divisional goals.

Each department's budget request must be based on the previous year's review, future goals and objectives, and the funding section of the CAS standards. Turek reported that increases in funding and personnel have directly resulted from working with the CAS standards.

Another very positive result of using the standards on the Adrian campus has been the establishment of new programs and employment of additional staff members. Turek used the standards to support the creation of minority affairs and counseling center positions. Finally, Turek introduced the CAS standards to the college's long-range planning committee, composed of faculty, administrators, and students. They responded positively to the document, and Turek believes the committee will use the standards in their planning process to help set the long-range agenda for the institution.

Why did the CAS standards have such a positive effect on the student affairs division at Adrian College? Foremost, the chief student affairs officer believed strongly in them. He found the standards to be an outstanding instructional tool and used them in an extensive staff development program.

In summary, Turek stated that he felt fortunate to be at an institution that accepted *CAS Standards and Guidelines* as an important document. He stated, "Obviously, the standards are not discussed on a daily basis; however, they do have the support of the president." Turek reported that he had extensively discussed the standards with the president and felt support from his fellow vice-presidents, the planning committee, and the student affairs division. He attributed this support to the success of the CAS authors in providing standards that are easily read, nonfrustrating, and nonthreatening or discouraging to any institution. Turek plans to use the standards on an annual basis and stated, "After this interview I might now try to find a few more ways to apply the CAS standards on my campus."

University of North Carolina at Wilmington

It was in May 1986 that two copies of *CAS Standards and Guidelines,* having arrived on the desk of the chancellor, were forwarded to the vice-chancellor for student affairs at the University of North Carolina at Wilmington (UNCW). William A. Bryan (personal communication, January 8, 1990), vice-chancellor for student affairs, personally returned one copy to the chancellor's office and scheduled a meeting with the chancellor to discuss the standards. When the two met, the only topic of discussion was the CAS standards. The chancellor decided to read the standards and meet again with Bryan. The second meeting produced a lengthy discussion and a charge to the Division of Student Affairs: Undertake a self-study and make specific recommendations based on the CAS standards and guidelines.

UNCW currently operationalizes the CAS standards as well as anyone in higher education (see Bryan and Mullendore, this volume). Following the chancellor's charge, the process of operationalization began. Small review teams made up of students, faculty, and staff members were assigned to review the functional areas. Each team was chaired by a student affairs professional from a functional area other than the one being examined. For example, the director of residence life chaired the group reviewing campus activities. Bryan was quick to point out that this method worked well at Wilmington, although this may not be true for all campuses. The key was involvement of appropriate constituencies: students, faculty, student affairs staff members, nondivisional staff members, and alumni.

The standards review process consisted of two broad charges: (1) review of the CAS standards and guidelines and the development of division standards statements for the functional areas in student affairs and (2) formulation of recommendations to assist functional areas in meeting stated standards.

Accomplishment of both tasks required a well-thought out plan. The teams were first briefed on the CAS standards. Included in this briefing was a historical perspective on CAS and an identification of the twenty-two professional associations that supported the standards. The general standards and the functional area standards and guidelines needed by each group were then distributed. Detailed discussion of the standards followed the distribution. Explanation of the differences between standards and the recommended guidelines was an essential part of the discussion, according to Associate Vice-Chancellor Richard Mullendore (personal communication, January 9, 1990). Mullendore headed the team that dealt with student orientation programs.

The teams began their interactive work by looking at their assigned CAS functional area statements. Teams were free to use any set of standards specific to the functional areas they were studying. Several functional areas such as counseling services, financial aid, and health services used other professional standards. Bryan insisted that group members have access to all available standards.

The comparison of each student affairs functional area to the respective standards and guidelines pointed out both strengths and weaknesses in the existing programs and services. The teams were expected to work on those identified problem areas and develop appropriate recommendations for improvement. Recommendations to bring each department or functional area into compliance with the standards were given to Bryan and each department head. Additionally, the recommendations were distributed widely on campus to different constituencies, and they became the planning document of the division for meeting or exceeding the published CAS standards.

The next step implemented by Bryan was to expand ownership of the standards on the Wilmington campus. Student affairs staff members reviewed the CAS standards and guidelines for different campus groups in several different forums. The UNCW Board of Trustees heard a detailed explanation of the continuing CAS standards review process and of future division plans in a presentation by Bryan. A similar presentation was made to the Faculty Senate: a question-and-answer format was used with the Student Senate. The inner circle of people who knew about the CAS standards and guidelines grew rapidly.

Immediately following the "spreading of the word," Bryan outlined for his division a CAS standards review process. Much like the earlier work groups, professional staff members reviewed their own functional areas against the CAS standards and guidelines. They also examined the self-study recommendations generated by the committees. Specific recommendations for each of the CAS components—mission, program, organization and administration, human resources, facilities, campus and community relations, funding, ethics, and evaluation—were presented to Bryan. After completion of this activity, he asked department heads to develop a UNCW standards statement for each functional area that included the following elements: (1) a written mission and program statement, (2) an updated organization chart and policy statement for each area, (3) an outline of human resources for each department, (4) an identification of available funding, (5) an identification and description of all physical facilities, (6) a discussion of relationships developed on or off campus by members of each department, (7) stated ethical standards, and (8) an identification of each department's evaluation process.

Each evaluation area standard statement was quite detailed and served as the planning document for that area and, ultimately, the division. The standard statement for the Student Orientation Program, headed by Mullendore, serves as a fine example. It opened with a one-paragraph mission statement, followed by a set of detailed goals subdivided into the major categories of institutional understanding, academic understanding, student transition, services, and opportunities. The program section referred directly to the CAS standards when describing an orientation program that included both academic and student life components, along with structured opportunities for interaction with different campus constituencies. Organizational and administrative components of the program were very detailed. Human resources were explained to the point of an exact salary breakdown from the director to clerical helpers. Student orientation leaders were included in the human resources section. The funding and facilities sections were likewise detailed. The campus and community relations area was frank in its discussion of internal politics, and the ethics section spoke strongly of student and staff adherence to the highest standards. Finally, the evaluation area spoke proudly of the summer-orientation evaluation process but stated there was a lack of evaluation for the spring and fall programs, as well as for the orientation leaders' training program.

Eighteen student affairs departments or functional areas at Wilmington now operate under similar statements based on the CAS standards and guidelines. The entire set of standards statements are reviewed annually by each department head. Also, Bryan has recently introduced a new planning cycle based on the maturing of the division's review process (see Bryan and Mullendore, this volume).

Bryan felt strongly that the CAS review process has moved the UNCW

Division of Student Affairs forward in the past five years. Support for the standards was always strong internally, but the most movement was made externally. Faculty and staff who knew very little about student affairs became increasingly supportive as a direct result of being involved in the self-study teams. Enough faculty were involved that the good word spread quickly. Bryan believed credibility was gained. More people now understand the mission of the Division of Student Affairs. Budgets have been increased with the support of the CAS review process, a prime example being disabled student services. Since the division's standards work began, institutional commitment has increased significantly in this area. Additionally, substantial competition for dollars has been created within the division. Bryan stated that staff members have learned to be more creative in gaining support for needed budget dollars, and "the result can only be better programs for the students."

Finally, Bryan indicated that the use of professional standards is an ongoing process at UNCW. In the past three years standards have been written for two areas not covered by CAS: leadership and substance abuse. These statements were designed according to the CAS format. Bryan closed the discussion by stating that "all work in the area of standards use at UNCW and nationwide should be considered to be an evolving draft document."

Summary

The utilization of student services standards is in its infancy. A number of professional associations have dominated the development process; however, more than three-quarters of the commonly accepted areas of student services have developed no standards separate from those incorporated in the CAS (1986) document. The literature reveals relatively little articulation of the essence of the field of student affairs. CAS is involved in the first truly profession-wide attempt to create and encourage utilization of student services and student development program standards. Meyer (1986) has documented practitioners' acceptance of the standards.

This chapter has presented several successful examples of application of the CAS standards and guidelines at seven postsecondary educational institutions, located in various regions of the country. Other standards documents published by various professional associations were included in the discussion. Use of professional standards in large and small colleges was examined, as well as in public and private institutions. The exciting aspect of collecting this information was discovering the creativity and diversity with which the standards are being used. The founding of a counseling center, the use of the document by a statewide task force, and the revision of a graduate curriculum all bear witness to the possible multiple applications of professional standards on campuses throughout the country.

Currently, use of the CAS standards and guidelines on college and university campuses is largely dependent on the interest and commitment of chief student affairs officers. This suggests that personal motivation is needed for initiatives to be implemented. The primary need is to increase awareness of the existence of professional standards. Appendix D of this volume provides a list of institutions and individual contact persons who are current users of the CAS standards. Increasing the visibility of professional standards must become a number-one priority among student affairs practitioners and their organizations. The CAS standards and guidelines, among other professional initiatives, deserve considered attention at all levels of professional endeavor. They provide an excellent tool for achieving the kind of successful practice to which all student affairs programs and personnel should aspire.

References

American Psychological Association (APA). *Psychological Manual.* (3rd ed.) Washington, D.C.: APA, 1983.

Association of College and University Housing Officers-International (ACUHO-I). *Statement of Standards.* Columbus, Ohio: ACUHO-I, 1985.

California State University (CSU). *Report of the Educational Support Services Master Plan Task Force.* Long Beach: CSU, 1989.

Council for the Advancement of Standards for Student Services/Development Programs (CAS). *CAS Standards and Guidelines for Student Services/Development Programs.* Washington, D.C.: CAS, 1986.

Meyer, H. T. "A National Effort to Build Standards for the Student Services/Development Functions: A Historical Analysis." Unpublished doctoral dissertation, Graduate School of Education, Department of Education Administration and Supervision, Rutgers University, 1986.

Miller, T. K., Thomas, W. L., Looney, S. C., and Yerian, J. *CAS Self Assessment Guides.* Washington, D.C.: Council for the Advancement of Standards for Student Services/Development Programs, 1988.

National Association of College and University Food Services (NACUFS). *Professional Standards Manual.* East Lansing, Mich.: NACUFS, 1986.

Joseph M. Marron is director of student support services at the North Carolina State Department of Community Colleges. He is a former chief student affairs officer with thirteen years experience in the field. He has conducted extensive research in the area of professional standards in student affairs.

Appendix A: Regional Institutional Accrediting Bodies

Middle States

Delaware, District of Columbia, Maryland, New Jersey, New York, Pennsylvania, Puerto Rico, Virgin Islands, and other geographical areas in which the commission now conducts accrediting activities.

Commission on Higher Education
Middle States Association of Colleges and Schools
Howard L. Simmons, Executive Director
3624 Market Street
Philadelphia, Pennsylvania 19104
(215) 662-5606

New England

Connecticut, Maine, Massachusetts, New Hampshire, Rhode Island, Vermont, and other geographical areas in which the commissions now conduct accrediting activities.

Commission on Institutions of Higher Education
New England Association of Schools and Colleges
Charles M. Cook, Director
The Sanborn House
15 High Street
Winchester, Massachusetts 01890
(617) 729-6762, FAX (617) 729-0924

Commission on Vocational, Technical, and Career Institutions
New England Association of Schools and Colleges
Daniel S. Maloney, Director of the Commission
The Sanborn House
15 High Street
Winchester, Massachusetts 01890
(617) 729-6762, FAX (617) 729-0924

North Central

Arizona, Arkansas, Colorado, Illinois, Indiana, Iowa, Kansas, Michigan, Minnesota, Missouri, Nebraska, New Mexico, North Dakota, Ohio, Oklahoma,

South Dakota, West Virginia, Wisconsin, Wyoming, and other geographical areas in which the commission now conducts accrediting activities.

Commission on Institutions of Higher Education
North Central Association of Colleges and Schools
Patricia A. Thrash, Executive Director
159 North Dearborn Street
Chicago, Illinois 60601
(312) 263-0456, 1-800-621-7440, FAX (312) 263-7462

Northwest

Alaska, Idaho, Montana, Nevada, Oregon, Utah, Washington, and other geographical areas in which the commission now conducts accrediting activities.

Commission on Colleges
Northwest Association of Schools and Colleges
Joseph A. Malik, Executive Director
3700-B University Way, N.E.
Seattle, Washington 98105
(206) 543-0195

Southern

Alabama, Florida, Georgia, Kentucky, Louisiana, Mississippi, North Carolina, South Carolina, Tennessee, Texas, Virginia, and other geographical areas in which the commissions now conduct accrediting activities.

Commission on Colleges
Southern Association of Colleges and Schools
James T. Rogers, Executive Director
1866 Southern Lane
Decatur, Georgia 30033-4097
(404) 329-6500, 1-800-248-7701, FAX (404) 329-6598

Commission on Occupational Education Institutions
Southern Association of Colleges and Schools
Kenneth W. Tidwell, Executive Director
1866 Southern Lane
Decatur, Georgia 30033-4097
(404) 329-6530, 1-800-248-7701, FAX (404) 329-6598

Western

California, Hawaii, Guam, and other geographical areas in which the commissions now conduct accrediting activities.

Accrediting Commission for Community and Junior Colleges

Western Association of Schools and Colleges

John C. Petersen, Executive Director
P. O. Box 70
9053 Soquel Drive
Aptos, California 95003
(408) 688-7575

Accrediting Commission for Senior Colleges and Universities

Western Association of Schools and Colleges

Stephen S. Weiner, Executive Director
P. O. Box 9990, Mills College
Oakland, California 94613-0990
(415) 632-5000

Appendix B: Specialized Accrediting Bodies

Accreditation Association for Ambulatory Health Care, Inc.
9933 Lawler Avenue
Skokie, Illinois 60077-3702
(708) 676-9610

American Psychological Association, Committee on Accreditation (COPA Member Agency)
Doctoral programs in professional specialties of psychology and predoctoral internship training programs in professional psychology
Paul D. Nelson, Director
Office of Accreditation
1200 Seventeenth Street, N.W.
Washington, D.C. 20036
(202) 955-7670

Council for Accreditation of Counseling and Related Educational Programs (COPA Member Agency)

American Association for Counseling and Development
Carol L. Bobby, Executive Director
5999 Stevenson Avenue
Alexandria, Virginia 22304
(703) 823-9800, FAX (703) 823-0252

International Association of Counseling Services
5999 Stevenson Avenue, 3rd Floor
Alexandria, Virginia 22304
(703) 832-9840

Joint Commission on Accreditation of Healthcare Organizations
1 Renaissance Boulevard
Oakbrook Terrace, Illinois 60181
(708) 916-5600

Appendix C: Professional Standards and Accrediting Agencies

Council for the Advancement of Standards for Student Services/Development Programs (CAS)

Office of Student Affairs
2108 Mitchell Building
University of Maryland at College Park
College Park, Maryland 20742-5221

Council on Postsecondary Accreditation (COPA)

1 Dupont Circle, N.W.
Suite 305
Washington, D.C. 20036
(202) 452-1433

Appendix D: Institutional Resource List for Current Users of CAS Standards

Adrian College, Adrian, Michigan
Robert Turek, Vice-President and Dean for Student Affairs
Bethel College, North Newton, Kansas
Ronald Fleming, Dean of Students
Carroll College, Waukesha, Wisconsin
Gary E. Kellom, Vice-President for Student Development
East Tennessee State University, Johnson City
Stephen Badar, Associate Vice-President for Student Affairs
Millersville University of Pennsylvania, Millersville
Gary Reighard, Vice-President for Student Affairs
Mississippi State University, Mississippi State
Gerald Tice, Assistant to the Vice-President for Student Affairs and Director of Housing and Residence Life
Morgan State University, Baltimore, Maryland
Raymond A. Downs, Vice-President for Student Affairs
North Carolina Wesleyan College, Rocky Mount
Joseph M. Marron, Dean of Student Life
Notre Dame College, Manchester, New Hampshire
Alicia Finn, Dean of Student Development
Rosemont College, Rosemont, Pennsylvania
Ethel C. Levenson, Dean of Students
Saint Norbert College, De Pere, Wisconsin
Richard Rankin, Vice-President for Student Affairs
Saint Olaf College, Northfield, Minnesota
Carol V. Johnson, Vice-President and Dean of Student Affairs
Sonoma State University, Rohnert Park, California
Rand Link, Dean of Student Affairs
Syracuse University, Syracuse, New York
Mary Jo Custer, Assistant to the Vice-President
University of North Carolina, Wilmington
William A. Bryan, Vice-Chancellor for Student Affairs
University of South Florida, Tampa
Charles F. Hewitt, Associate Vice-President for Student Affairs
University of Wisconsin, LaCrosse
Reid Horle, Dean of Student Development and Coordinator of the College Student Personnel Program

Virginia Military Institute, Lexington
Royce E. Jones, Director of Cadet Affairs
Washington State University, Pullman
Maureen Anderson, Vice-President for Student Affairs

INDEX

Ordering Information

New Directions for Student Services is a series of paperback books that offers guidelines and programs for aiding students in their total development—emotional, social, and physical, as well as intellectual. Books in the series are published quarterly in Fall, Winter, Spring, and Summer and are available for purchase by subscription as well as by single copy.

Subscriptions for 1991 cost $45.00 for individuals (a savings of 20 percent over single-copy prices) and $60.00 for institutions, agencies, and libraries. Please do not send institutional checks for personal subscriptions. Standing orders are accepted.

Single copies cost $13.95 when payment accompanies order. (California, New Jersey, New York, and Washington, D.C., residents please include appropriate sales tax.) Billed orders will be charged postage and handling.

Discounts for quantity orders are available. Please write to the address below for information.

All orders must include either the name of an individual or an official purchase order number. Please submit your order as follows:

Subscriptions: specify series and year subscription is to begin
Single copies: include individual title code (such as SS1)

Mail all orders to:
Jossey-Bass Inc., Publishers
350 Sansome Street
San Francisco, California 94104

For sales outside of the United States contact:
Maxwell Macmillan International Publishing Group
866 Third Avenue
New York, New York 10022

Other Titles Available in the
New Directions for Student Services Series
Margaret J. Barr, Editor-in-Chief; *M. Lee Upcraft*, Associate Editor

SS52 Affirmative Action on Campus, *Joseph G. Ponterotto, Diane E. Lewis, Robin Bullington*
SS51 Evolving Theoretical Perspectives on Students, *Leila V. Moore*
SS50 Community Service as Values Education, *Cecilia I. Delve, Suzanné D. Mintz, Greig M. Stewart*
SS49 Crisis Intervention and Prevention, *Harold L. Pruett, Vivian B. Brown*
SS48 Designing Campus Activities to Foster a Sense of Community, *Dennis C. Roberts*
SS47 Responding to Violence on Campus, *Jan M. Sherrill, Dorothy G. Siegel*
SS46 Religion on Campus, *John Butler*
SS45 Dealing with the Behavioral and Psychological Problems of Students, *Ursula Delworth*
SS44 Empowering Women: Leadership Development Strategies on Campus, *Mary Ann Danowitz Sagaria*
SS43 Performance Appraisal as a Tool for Staff Development, *Robert D. Brown*
SS42 Changing Roles for Men on Campus, *Ronald J. May, Murray Scher*
SS41 Managing Student Affairs Effectively, *M. Lee Upcraft, Margaret J. Barr*
SS40 Fraternities and Sororities on the Contemporary College Campus, *Roger B. Winston, Jr., William R. Nettles III, John H. Opper, Jr.*
SS39 Enhancing Campus Judicial Systems, *Robert Caruso, Will W. Travelstead*
SS38 Responding to the Needs of Today's Minority Students, *Doris J. Wright*
SS37 Expanding Opportunities for Professional Education, *Leila V. Moore, Robert B. Young*
SS36 Guiding the Development of Foreign Students, *K Richard Pyle*
SS35 Alcohol and the College Student, *Thomas G. Goodale*
SS34 Developing Campus Recreation and Wellness Programs, *Fred Leafgren*
SS33 Enhancing Relationships with the Student Press, *John H. Schuh*
SS32 Working with the Parents of College Students, *Robert D. Cohen*
SS31 Coping with Death on Campus, *Ellen S. Zinner*
SS30 Applied Ethics in Student Services, *Harry J. Canon, Robert D. Brown*
SS29 Facilitating the Development of Women, *Nancy J. Evans*
SS28 Rethinking Services for College Athletes, *Arthur Shriberg, Frederick R. Brodzinski*
SS27 Students as Paraprofessional Staff, *Steven C. Ender, Roger B. Winston, Jr.*
SS26 Enhancing Student Development with Computers, *Cynthia S. Johnson, K Richard Pyle*
SS25 Orienting Students to College, *M. Lee Upcraft*
SS24 Commuter Students: Enhancing Their Educational Experiences, *Sylvia S. Stewart*
SS23 Understanding Student Affairs Organizations, *George D. Kuh*
SS22 Student Affairs and the Law, *Margaret J. Barr*
SS21 Helping Students Manage Stress, *Elizabeth M. Altmaier*
SS20 Measuring Student Development, *Gary R. Hanson*
SS19 Mentoring-Transcript Systems for Promoting Student Growth, *Robert D. Brown, David A. DeCoster*
SS17 Developmental Approaches to Academic Advising, *Roger B. Winston, Jr., Steven C. Ender, Theodore K. Miller*
SS16 Understanding Today's Students, *David DeCoster, Phyllis Mable*